Daniel B Lancaster

You're Not Too Broken

Finding Jesus When Life Feels Beyond Repair

ISBN (Paperback): 978-1-968232-00-9
ISBN (Hardcover): 978-1-968232-01-6
For inquiries or permissions:
lightkeeperbooks.com

For Craig and Scott,
who showed me the way
by sitting with me in the dark—
and never rushing the light.

TABLE OF CONTENTS

Foreword

Have you discovered this principle? *What you don't talk out, you act out.* Like a pebble in your shoe producing a limp, what's emotionally or spiritually unaddressed always finds another way out.

It isn't just in a game of poker that we read body language for a "tell." We can see others are struggling or pinched or plagued by the unspoken. It comes out. The "tell" is in playing with the ring as he wrestles with a commitment, or twirling a lock of hair when she's feeling inferior. These actions signal there's something "else" that's unspoken and unaddressed.

In his book *You're Not Too Broken,* Dan invites you like a friend to sit down and rest a minute. Untie the shoe. Let that affliction come tumbling out. He guides you into a warm welcoming space to address the unaddressed. You need read no further than his introduction and you'll hear the invitation to meet Jesus who is waiting for you.

There's encouragement on every page. The welcome doesn't sour as you read. There's no "Gotcha!" only "I get you." I found it personally healing and helpful.

The right-sized chapters are a soothing read saturated with prayer and scriptures. They reveal God's tenderhearted love page by page. They're truly creating a rhythm that restores one's soul. In fact, the prayers lace the book like handrails down a dark stairway. They supply words where one's heart may be groping. They give an assurance that lifts the head and heart in grace to trust God in what one's facing and releasing.

The first half of the book is the heart. It's pulsing with life-giving truths—like white blood cells carrying healing. You will feel recovery happening.

Yet there's more.

As you travel the solid stairway into your soul, you'll find that the second half of the book is where the breathing deepens. It's where the truths you've read begin to settle into practice—into prayer, reflection, and sacred rhythm. That portion isn't just helpful. It's like the lungs. Turn those pages and find yourself drawing in deep breaths of air that resuscitate you with gospel truths.

Read it for yourself, and see if you don't feel compelled to share them with others. They are life-giving. They are oxygen for the soul.

Are you willing to begin? You'll find it worth it. Jesus invites you—come weary, leave rested.

With prayers for you to meet Jesus in fresh ways,

Alan Malchuk, Licensed Clinical Social Worker
SureCord Christian Counseling
Ecclesiastes 4:12

Preface

If you're holding this book, something in you is stirring. Maybe it's grief. Maybe it's a question you've been carrying for a while. Maybe it's just a quiet sense that something's not quite settled in your soul.

This is a book for that.

It's not a fix. It's not a formula. It's an invitation to begin again—slowly, honestly, with Jesus present in every room of your story.

I didn't write these pages as someone with answers. I wrote them as someone still healing too. Someone who's had to learn, again and again, how to live with a soft heart. How to open one door at a time.

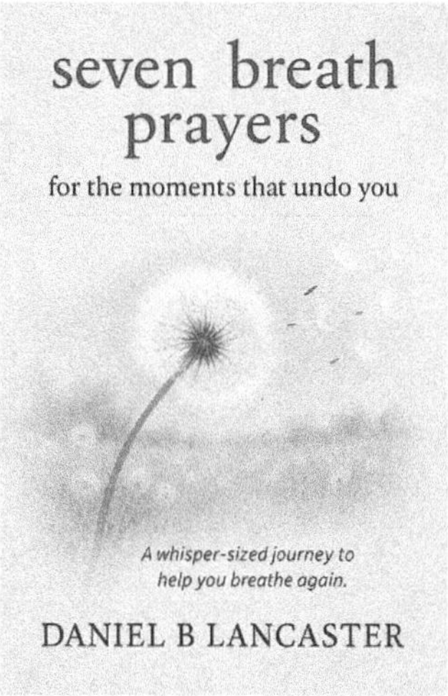

seven breath prayers
for the moments that undo you
A whisper-sized journey to help you breathe again.
DANIEL B LANCASTER

As you begin, I want to offer you a simple gift:

seven breath prayers for the moments that undo you

You can download it at: https://go.lkbooks.net/7PrayersSignUp

It's free, and it's yours. These are whisper-sized prayers—one-line ways to breathe when you feel overwhelmed, ashamed, afraid, or unsure what to say. Keep them in your pocket. Save them on your phone. Return to them when words run dry.

Whether or not you use the prayer guide, my prayer is this:

That you would not give up. That you would keep the soil of your heart soft. That you would come to believe—deep in your bones—you are not too broken for healing.

Not too broken for God. Not too broken for love. Not too broken to begin again.

I'm grateful you're here. Let's walk this out together.

—Dan

Prologue

We all know that feeling—being surrounded, yet somehow unseen. Think of a moment in a crowded room. Maybe it's a church service, the air thick with hymns, or a family gathering, buzzing with conversations. Yet, a strange isolation settles over you—like watching life instead of living it. Not just silence, but a hollow ache that hints at something missing deep inside.

A tightness grips your throat. Breathing takes effort. Your limbs feel heavy, like gravity has doubled. And all around you, life swirls effortlessly for others. But not for you. Have you ever felt that paradox? Surrounded by activity but painfully alone?

You go through your day—a practiced rhythm of smiles and conversations—while an ache quietly hums beneath the surface, a low chord of weariness. It follows you through meetings and meals, a tension you can't quite name. It's not just exhaustion. It's a hunger for something real. A connection that fills the gap. You whisper to yourself, *"Is this all there is?"*

I've been there.

I've sat with people who appear strong on the outside—missionaries, leaders, parents, professionals—who lower their voices and say, *"There's a hollowness inside."* A dryness of spirit. A quiet grief that shapes everything. And when they say it, something inside you nods—even if your mouth stays closed.

Maybe that grief echoes in you, too. You keep up with responsibilities. You meet expectations. But there's a shadow under the song of your life.

But what if that ache isn't a sign of God's absence? What if it's the place He's already drawing near—through Jesus, the One who steps into every ache and offers peace?

What if the emptiness you feel isn't a verdict against you—but an open doorway? A holy invitation into the rooms of your heart where old wounds whisper and deferred dreams still breathe, waiting to be seen, named, and healed.

What if God, in His deep mercy, is already waiting there?

Our hearts are like old houses. Some rooms are full of light—laughter, joy, and memories that warm us. Others stay locked—rooms with pain, loss, regret. And yet, the whole house matters. Jesus doesn't just visit the tidy parts. He wants to dwell in all of it—every hallway, every locked door.

We learn to avoid those rooms. Build our lives around them. Pretend they don't exist. But the echoes remain.

And yet, healing doesn't mean tearing down the house. Healing means courage.

It means choosing to open the door, walk into those forgotten rooms, and discover we are not alone.

Because Jesus has promised: *"I will never leave you nor forsake you."* And that includes the spaces where we feel most abandoned.

He is already there...steady, patient, kind. He isn't afraid of the mess. He doesn't flinch. He enters even the coldest corners with warmth.

This book is for anyone tired of pretending. For those weary of surface living. For those ready to walk with God into the deeper places.

It won't give you a checklist. It won't demand perfection. It will offer a path.

A path that starts by listening to the whispers of your heart. That moves through inner restoration. That leads toward authentic connection—with God, with others, and with yourself.

You'll learn how to walk this healing path:

- *Attend to the Whispers* – Recognize emotions as messengers, not threats.
- *Reclaim the Inner Landscape* – Explore your heart with courage and kindness.
- *Build Bridges of Connection* – Move toward grace-filled relationships.
- *Compose a Symphony of Wholeness* – Let God weave your whole story into something redemptive.

God isn't grading you, He's walking with you. It's about being present with Him.

The same Jesus who walked through walls to reach fearful disciples still enters locked rooms today—rooms we thought we had to keep hidden. And when He enters, He brings peace, like morning light streaming through a dusty window, soft and steady.

So take a breath.
Drop the weight of self-judgment.

This moment doesn't ask for perfection—just presence.
You are not beyond hope.
You are not beyond healing.

Let this be the moment you open the door.

Reflection Prompts:
What rooms of your heart have you been avoiding?
What would it look like to invite Jesus into one of them today?

This isn't a question to fix—just one to carry as you begin.

Let's begin this journey.
Not alone, but together.

With Jesus.
Always with Jesus.

You don't have to know the whole path.
You just have to take one honest step.

Part 1

Why Healing Is Essential

Before we jump into the how, we need to spend a little time with the why.

Why does this ache keep returning?
Why does healing matter if we're already forgiven?
Why do we feel so tired—even when we believe?

These aren't questions to fix.
They're invitations to feel.

This part is about naming the ache.
About making space for honesty.

Because healing doesn't begin with answers.
It begins with presence.

Chapter 1

Your Wounds Aren't the End of the Story

A young woman once told me, "I feel like a ghost in my own life." Maybe you've felt that too—maybe you're there right now. You're showing up, keeping things together. People think you're fine. But something feels off. Numb. Tired. Quietly unraveling.

You've prayed. You've read the verses. You've whispered, *"I should be okay by now."* But the ache lingers.

What if that ache isn't proof that God has left you... but the place He's meeting you?

What if your pain isn't the end of your story—but the place where healing begins?

Blessed are the poor in spirit,
for theirs is the kingdom of heaven.
—*Matthew 5:3*—

You're Not Alone

If you've ever felt spiritually flat, emotionally exhausted, or like you're falling apart inside your own skin... you're not the only one.

I've walked with pastors, single moms, professionals, and faithful believers who quietly say, *"I'm not okay."*

A construction worker, worn from years of labor, once confessed, "I feel broken in places no one sees."

A vibrant immigrant mother, always serving others, whispered, "I feel invisible. Like I don't matter."

A retired teacher, after decades of pouring into students, said, "There's still an emptiness I can't explain. And I love Jesus. But it's still there."

This ache wears different faces. But it often sounds like this:

- You're always giving, but feel spiritually dry.
- You smile in public, but collapse in private.
- You feel ashamed for struggling—even though you believe in grace.
- You've "moved on" from things that still bleed in silence.

This isn't weakness. It's the weight of being human in a broken world. And Jesus sees it all.

When the Church Goes Silent

Somewhere along the way, we confused salvation with perfection. We believed being saved meant being okay.

So, when we weren't okay—we hid it.

We buried sorrow. We silenced doubt. We sang the songs with tears behind our eyes. All the while, Jesus stood nearby—unafraid of our questions, unshaken by our grief, and willing to heal what we didn't know we could bring to Him.

A young man once said, "I thought my doubts made me a bad Christian."

A woman shared, "I was told to choose joy, so I stopped talking about my pain."

But healing doesn't begin with *pretending*. It begins with *presence*. And Jesus is not offended by yours.

What Healing Really Looks Like

Healing isn't the same as fixing. Fixing is fast, external, surface-level. Healing is slower, internal, and sacred.

Fixing patches the cracks, but healing restores the foundation. Fixing focuses on control—healing happens through surrender.

Jesus isn't the Great Problem-Solver. He's the Great Physician. He doesn't just repair. He renews.

He meets you in the ache. He stays with you in the silence. And He walks with you—not to hurry you, but to heal you.

And here's where grace comes in:

- God's saving grace forgives your sin.
- God's sustaining grace heals your wounds.

Both are gifts. Both flow from love. And neither depends on you having it all together.

And healing rarely happens in isolation. Sometimes Jesus brings it through community—safe people who sit with us, remind us we're not alone, and reflect His presence.

What This Book Will (and Won't) Do

You won't find a spiritual to-do list here. You won't be told your pain is your fault. You won't be pushed to try harder.

Instead, you'll find:

- A biblical path to inner healing that you can return to again and again
- Six core steps based on the vowels—A-E-I-O-U-Y—each rooted in the Beatitudes
- A healing rhythm, not a formula—gentle, honest, and grounded in grace

This isn't a race. It's a rhythm. And Jesus is already walking it with you. You don't need strength to start. Just the courage to be real.

A Turning Point

I remember sitting in my car, the engine off, hands on the steering wheel. The air was still. My hands gripped the wheel, more to stay grounded than to drive.

My life looked fine—on paper. Ministry, family, faith. But inside? I was tired in a way sleep couldn't touch.

I whispered, "Jesus, I don't know what's wrong. But I can't fake this anymore."

That moment didn't change everything overnight—but it changed *something*. I felt seen. Held. A tiny shift from surviving... to healing.

That's what I hope this book becomes for you. Not a miracle cure. But a gentle turning point.

A quiet yes to healing.

A Gentle Invitation

This book isn't about arriving. It's about returning. To God. To yourself. To the parts of your heart you had to shut down just to survive.

If you've been carrying things too heavy for too long, this is your invitation to lay them down. You're not broken beyond repair. You are loved into restoration.

Readiness isn't the requirement, willingness is. And you're here now.

You're right on time. Healing begins here.

Live It Out

Don't rush past this moment. Take a breath. Then take a moment to reflect:

- What chapter of your story have you labeled "too messy"—

  when it might actually be God's invitation into deeper healing?
- What would it look like to bring that part into the light with Jesus?
- Write down one sentence that begins with: *"Maybe healing could begin where..."* and finish it honestly.

This isn't about fixing everything. It's about being open to something new. And you've already taken the first step.

A Prayer for the Weary

Lord Jesus,

For those souls weary and hollow, I lift them up now.

Like the ones in this chapter, they carry a weight that sleep cannot lift, a disconnection that whispers, "Is this all there is?"

I pray for my friend, [insert name], burdened by unspoken grief, feeling unseen.

May Your presence meet them. May they know this emptiness is but a doorway to Your deeper love.

As You met the brokenhearted, lift their heads.

In Your name, Amen.

Coming Up Next

Naming the ache instead of hiding it—that's already a brave first step. But what if that ache is more than pain? What if it's a message, a soul-deep signal that something sacred has come unplugged?

In the next chapter, we'll go beneath the surface. Not just to examine symptoms like anxiety, shame, or numbness—but to explore the quieter disconnections that often go unnamed: disconnection from God, from others, and even from yourself.

This isn't about blame. It's about becoming whole.

❦

I see you. I've always seen you. —Jesus

Chapter 2
What's Really Hurting You?

You show up. You try your best. You check the boxes of a faithful life. But still—something inside feels foggy. Like a radio slightly off station. You hear the music, but it's not quite clear. You feel tired in a way rest doesn't fix. Overwhelmed. Second-guessing yourself. Not broken—but not okay either.

I remember sitting in the church parking lot, watching families walk in. Smiles, handshakes, Sunday shoes. But inside me? A quiet ache. Not for lack of faith—but for lack of connection.

And that's terrifying, isn't it? Especially when you've been walking with Jesus for a while. Especially when you've told others how good God is. Especially when you're the strong one. The leader. The encourager.

So, instead of asking for help, you keep going. You push through. You manage. But here's what I want to tell you:

You're not failing. You're disconnected.

You're not the only one feeling this. It looks different for everyone—but the ache is real:

A successful businessman battling burnout realized, "My drive masked a deep fear of inadequacy." A devoted stay-at-home mother admitted, "I'm terrified that if I stop performing, I'll disappear." A first-generation college student confessed, "I feel like I'm betraying my family and failing to fit in at the same time."

Disconnection wears many faces. But God's not angry. He's drawing near.

Even to your old age and gray hairs I am he, I am he who will sustain you.
—Isaiah 46:4—

The Message of Pain

We often perceive pain as an adversary—something to be avoided, suppressed, or quickly overcome. But what if pain isn't your enemy at all?

What if it's a messenger—a flashing warning light that something in your soul is unplugged? You're not broken because you're hurting. You're human. And like every human soul, you were created for connection.

When connection breaks—when the soul's cord frays—we lose more than energy. We lose clarity. We lose peace. We lose the sense that God is near, others are safe, or that we ourselves are worth caring for.

We get tired of pretending we're fine—and we lose our footing. That's when the vicious cycles start.

A young artist once told me, "It feels like there's static in my soul—like I'm trying to tune in to God, but the signal keeps breaking up."

An elderly widower called it "a deep loneliness that even church can't touch."

A single father said it was "like living with a ghost of myself, numb and going through the motions."

Three Core Disconnections

To understand how disconnection hurts, we need to see what connection was meant to be. Behind the burnout. Beneath the overreactions.

Underneath the cycles of shame, fear, or exhaustion...there's almost always a loss of connection in one of these three places:

1. Disconnection from God

You still believe. You still pray. But there's a wall you can't name. You might feel like:

- God is real, but silent
- You're not sure He's listening
- You're performing for Him, not walking with Him

This kind of disconnection often forms slowly. Sometimes from disappointment—when prayers go unanswered. Sometimes from religious trauma—when God was used as a weapon. Sometimes from unprocessed grief—when we stop talking to Him because we don't want to admit how mad or scared we really are.

But here's the truth:

God hasn't pulled away. He's drawing closer. He is *"near to the brokenhearted"* (Psalm 34:18). He invites the weary and burdened to come, not perform (Matthew 11:28).

He's not offended by your silence.
He's already waiting in it.

2. Disconnection from Others

You love people—but you don't trust easily. You're friendly—but no one really knows you. You're constantly pouring out, but feel invisible when you run dry.

This kind of disconnection often comes from betrayal, abandonment, or deep grief. You learned that it's safer to withdraw than risk rejection.

So, you keep relationships shallow or one-sided. Or you live in constant fear of letting someone down. But God never meant for you to carry this alone. In fact, healing requires a safe community.

Paul says, *"Carry each other's burdens..."* (Galatians 6:2). James writes, *"Confess your sins to each other and pray for each other so that you may be healed"* (James 5:16).

We don't heal in isolation. We heal when grace—that undeserved favor and love from God, like a hand reaching out to help you up when you're falling—flows through real, human connection.

I think of a woman from a culture where vulnerability was seen as weakness. She poured her heart out in a support group and later said, "For the first time, I felt seen and accepted, not in spite of my pain, but because of it." *Connection shattered her isolation.*

3. Disconnection from Self

This one is the hardest to see—and the easiest to ignore.

You stay busy so you don't have to think. You're hard on yourself in ways you'd never be with anyone else. You don't really know what you feel anymore—or what you need.

Somewhere along the way, you learned that your feelings were too much. That your needs made you a burden. That your worth was tied to your usefulness.

So, you perform. Perfect. Push down the mess. But it always surfaces.

But it doesn't stay buried. It shows up in anxiety, shame, confusion, and emotional exhaustion.

Here's what's true: You were created in the image of God (Genesis 1:27). And that includes your emotions, your wiring, your desires.

Jesus didn't just come to rescue your soul—He came to restore your identity. Loving yourself isn't selfish. It's part of the second greatest commandment: *"Love your neighbor as yourself" (Mark 12:31).*

Remember, being created in God's image doesn't mean we look exactly like Him, but that we share His ability to love, create, and feel—so disconnecting from ourselves is like ignoring a core part of who He made us to be.

Signs of Disconnection

Sometimes disconnection is quiet. But it still speaks. Loudly. Here's what it might be saying:

- You avoid silence because you're afraid of what will surface
- You find yourself reacting way too strongly to small things
- You're constantly comparing, competing, or criticizing
- You know how to help others—but feel stuck in your own struggles

None of this means you're failing. It means something's missing.

The Original Design

Before sin ever entered the world, God created connection. Adam walked with God. Eve was given as a companion. They were "naked and unashamed"—fully known, fully seen, fully loved.

Then came the rupture. Sin shattered connection. Shame entered. Blame followed. Hiding began.

But Jesus came to reverse it all. Not just to forgive—but to restore. He reconnects us to the Father. He places us in family. He teaches us to live in truth, not masks.

Healing isn't about being *fixed*—it's about being *reconnected.* To God. To others. To yourself.

This was always God's design: not just fixing what's broken—but reconnecting what's been lost.

Time to Reflect

Before we move forward into healing, we need to name what's really hurting us.

Healing starts with naming what's true. Not to fix it—but to face it.

Ask yourself:

- Where do I feel most distant right now—God, others, or myself?
- What emotion do I avoid the most—and why?
- What mask have I been wearing just to feel safe?
- What's the loudest message my pain is sending me?
- Where have I felt unplugged lately?

Name one person you trust—could you share one of these answers with them? And then pray, simply and honestly:

Jesus,

I don't always understand what's going on inside me. But I want You to come closer.

I want to feel connected again—really connected.

To You. To people. To myself.

Show me where to begin. I'm open.

In Your name, Amen.

A Prayer for the Disconnected

Dear Jesus,

For those wrestling with disconnection, I come to You. Those who strive to believe, to pray, yet feel a wall, a static in their spirit.

I think of [insert name], who masks their pain, feeling unseen, doubting if even You truly see.

Lord, draw near to the brokenhearted, remind them they're not alone, that You see their pain.

Soften their hearts, help them trust Your unwavering presence.

In Your name, Amen.

Coming Up Next

In the next part, we'll walk through the actual steps Jesus gives us for healing—hidden in plain sight in the Beatitudes.

These steps aren't about achievement—they're about invitation.

One vowel at a time.

You were made for connection—and the healing starts here.

❦

You've come further than you think. —Jesus

Part 2

Daily Invitations into God's Healing Presence

This is where it gets tender.
Not rushed. Not rigid.
Just one sacred step at a time.

Over the next seven days, you'll walk a gentle path—rooted in Jesus' words and guided by grace.

Each day holds space for reflection, connection, and quiet presence. Not to fix yourself. But to meet God where you are.

This isn't about doing more—it's about being known.
Like walking a quiet path with Someone who already knows the way.

You don't have to be ready. Just willing.

Let's begin—together, with Him.

I'm still holding what you've handed me. —Jesus

Chapter 3
The Healing Pathway

I used to read the Beatitudes like a checklist for "real Christians." Be poor in spirit. Mourn. Be meek. Hunger for righteousness.

It felt impossible. And honestly... exhausting.

But what if Jesus wasn't laying out a list of virtues to master? What if He was offering us a map to healing? What if the Beatitudes weren't about trying harder—but about opening wider?

These aren't commands. They're invitations.

Jesus didn't begin His most famous sermon by telling people how to behave—He began by blessing their brokenness. And that's where your healing begins, too.

A New Way to Hear the Beatitudes

Let's read them again—but this time, with a different lens. As you read, don't try to analyze. Just let them speak to the part of you that's still healing.

Blessed are the poor in spirit,
for theirs is the kingdom of heaven.

Blessed are those who mourn,
for they will be comforted.

Blessed are the meek,
for they will inherit the earth.

Blessed are those who hunger and thirst for
righteousness, for they will be filled.

Blessed are the merciful,
for they will be shown mercy.

Blessed are the pure in heart,
for they will see God.

Blessed are the peacemakers,
for they will be called children of God.
—Matthew 5:3–9—

What if these blessings weren't steps to climb, but gentle handholds—each one feeding the next like streams into a river? What if each one flowed gently into the next, like streams feeding the same river of restoration?

The truth is these blessings match the rhythm of inner healing. They begin in poverty of spirit and end in peacemaking.

That's why this book is structured around the six core steps of healing—A-E-I-O-U-Y—each linked to one of these Beatitudes.

You don't need a formula. Just a rhythm you can breathe. Because healing, like speaking, begins with breath. And every vowel helps us breathe.

Vowels = Breath = Healing Language

The Six Steps of the Healing Pathway

The Beatitudes aren't a to-do list for the super-spiritual. They're whispered invitations into the kind of healing we all need.

Each one isn't a gold star—it's a heart cry. And together, they map the journey from brokenness to wholeness.

A – Admit the Pain

Blessed are the poor in spirit...

What does it mean to be poor in spirit? It's not weakness, but a stark honesty, isn't it? That moment we finally confess, "*God, I'm empty,*" and in that very admission, the kingdom of heaven opens its doors.

E – Empathize with Yourself and Others

Blessed are those who mourn...

Why this blessing on mourning? Because we can't bypass the ache and expect to heal. It's not about wallowing, but honoring what was lost, allowing the tears to flow, so that comfort can flood in—for ourselves, and for those who mourn beside us.

I – Invite Jesus In

Blessed are the meek...

Ah, meekness. Such a misunderstood word. It's not weakness, but strength brought under control. It's the quiet courage to unlock those guarded places within and whisper, "Jesus, have access to this too," trusting that His presence is the most potent medicine.

O – Own What's Yours

Blessed are those who hunger and thirst for righteousness...

And now, a turning. We stop the blame game. We quit playing victim. We take responsibility. Not for the wounds inflicted, but for how we've chosen to respond. It's a fierce yearning for alignment, for setting things right, within and without. And that desire—God promises—it will be filled.

U – Understand the Story Behind the Struggle

Blessed are the merciful...

Mercy... it dawns with understanding, doesn't it? When we trace the lines of our own hurt, when we see the hidden scars in others, judgment softens. Compassion rises. And grace flows more freely.

It's here that we stop punishing ourselves and others—and start listening to what the pain has been trying to say.

Y – Yield to Healing

Blessed are the pure in heart...

Purity. Undivided devotion. No more masks. No more divided loyalties. Just surrender. Letting go. Trusting the Potter's hands to reshape what's been broken.

We stop resisting. We stop trying to fix ourselves. And we yield—to grace, to love, to Him. We welcome the healing presence of Jesus to do what only He can do.

The Outcome – Become a Peacemaker

Blessed are the peacemakers...

When you walk this healing path, you become something new.

You carry peace into rooms that used to trigger you. You speak gently to people you used to resent. You sit with others in their pain without trying to fix them.

You become a peacemaker—not because you're perfect, but because you've been healed.

And healed people carry peace wherever they go.

From Breakdown to Peace

A woman I once coached—let's call her Ana—was a high-functioning ministry leader. Respected, reliable, always ready to help. But privately, she felt invisible and overwhelmed.

She started this healing journey reluctantly. At first, just naming her exhaustion (A - Admit) felt like failure. But she stayed. She allowed herself to grieve years of loss and unmet needs (E - Empathize).

Then one afternoon, she whispered in prayer, "Jesus, I don't want to hide anymore" (I - Invite). That moment didn't erase the pain—but it cracked something open. A place where Jesus could come in.

She took responsibility for her emotional walls (O - Own), traced them back to a childhood where she was never allowed to need anything (U - Understand), and slowly let Jesus meet her in that abandoned space (Y - Yield).

Months later, her voice was different—gentler, freer. She wasn't "fixed." But she was healing. And she had become a safe place for others to begin healing, too.

A Prayer for the Hurting

Merciful Jesus,

For all who hurt, exhausted from trying to be strong, I pray.

For those like [insert name], feeling far from You, questioning Your awareness of their suffering.

Meet them in their honesty, Lord.

Draw near as they admit their need. Grant them comfort and strength as they walk this healing path with You, step by step.

In Your name, Amen.

A Gentle Summary and Invitation

You don't need to master this today. Or tomorrow. This is a rhythm, not a race. You'll come back to these steps again and again—and each time, they'll meet you in a new way.

Healing isn't a race—it's a rhythm. And you're not walking it alone.

In the next part of this book, we'll take one day for each step. Each day includes a scripture, a short reflection, some questions, and a quiet invitation to walk with Jesus.

You don't have to be ready. You just have to be willing. Which step feels hardest for you right now? Which one do you sense Jesus inviting you to take next?

So, if you're ready—even just a little—take His hand.

So let's begin—not perfectly, but honestly. One breath. One step. Together.

❖

Inhale: I bring all I am...

Exhale: To the One who holds all I need.

Day 1 – *Admit the Pain*

Blessed are the poor in spirit,
for theirs is the kingdom of heaven.
—Matthew 5:3—

He stood in the back of the sanctuary, long after the service had ended. Chairs were half-stacked. A few voices lingered in the hallway. But he remained—shoulders slumped, eyes tired, staring at the cross on the far wall. His body sagged. His spirit more so.

From the outside, he was reliable. Dependable. Always willing to help. But inside? Something had gone quiet.

That moment felt like failure, didn't it? But now we know—it was holy. Because it was honest. And that's the shift this whole journey begins with—not pretending, but naming what's real.

The Kingdom Begins in Poverty

Blessed are the poor in spirit...

It's the first sentence of Jesus' most famous sermon. And maybe the most misunderstood.

"Poor in spirit" doesn't mean weak or unmotivated. It means we finally stop performing and start admitting we need help. It means spiritually bankrupt—nothing left to offer, nothing left to hide.

Not impressive. Not performing. Just... open.

Jesus starts here because this is where every healing journey must begin. Not with power. Not with answers.

But with an ache and an admission: *"I can't do this anymore."*

This kind of honesty isn't a failure of faith—it's the seed of restoration.

Why We Struggle to Be Honest

We've learned to stay strong. To keep smiling. Especially in church. Somewhere along the way, many of us absorbed the message: *"Don't let them see you fall apart."*

So we hide—from others, from God, even from ourselves. But strength without honesty hardens into self-protection. And over time, that isolation costs us more than we know.

That's not healing. That's survival.

And survival isn't the same thing as being whole.

God Doesn't Heal What We Pretend Doesn't Hurt

Here's the truth: God is not looking for your polished prayers or curated persona. He's waiting for your unfiltered heart.

He doesn't require you to be okay. He just asks you to be real. If you're wondering whether God really welcomes you in this state, listen to what He's already said:

The Lord is close to the brokenhearted and
saves those who are crushed in spirit.
—Psalm 34:18—

A broken and contrite heart You will not
despise.
—Psalm 51:17—

Come to Me, all who are weary...
—Matthew 11:28—

God never rejects the honest cry. And He never turns away the one who's run out of strength.

You don't have to fix it. Just admit it.

Before & After

You wake up with that weight again. Not just tired—empty. Everything looks fine, but inside? You're fading.

You know what this feels like—not just in theory, but in your bones. You go through the motions—church, work, family—but it's like a radio playing in another room. You hear the sounds, but you're not really present. Prayers feel like words bouncing off the ceiling. The Bible feels like ink on paper. You're holding it together, but a quiet question keeps echoing: Is this all there is?

And then, one day, you pause. You let the weight settle and whisper, "I'm tired. I'm not okay."

In that moment, something shifts. The silence isn't empty anymore—it becomes a space where God can finally draw near. You remember that Jesus didn't come for the strong, but for the brokenhearted. And you realize—you're in good company.

The pressure breaks. Just a little. And honesty begins to trickle through.

Reflection Questions

Take a moment to reflect. Let your soul breathe. Write or whisper your answers—whatever helps you be honest.

What pain have I been hiding—from God, others, or myself?

Where have I tried to "stay strong" instead of being real?

What would I say to Jesus if I believed He wouldn't shame me for it?

A Breath Prayer

Find a quiet moment. Take a few deep breaths. Then, pray slowly with your inhale and exhale:

Inhale: Jesus, I have nothing left...

Exhale: ...But You are everything I need.

Repeat this two or three times, letting it sink in. This is how we pray when we're too tired to perform.

Healing Practice

Write a one-sentence truth in your journal or phone.

Example: *"God, I don't feel okay—and I'm tired of pretending I do."*

Sit in silence for two minutes. Don't rush. Let yourself be in God's presence—without fixing, hiding, or editing.

Place your hand over your heart and whisper—or simply think—these words... *"I am safe to be honest with God."*

That may seem small. But it's holy. It's the first step on the healing path.

A Closing Prayer

Jesus,

I don't have it all together.

I'm tired of pretending I do.

I've held it in for so long, afraid of being seen as weak. But You say the kingdom belongs to the poor in spirit. So, here I am.

Not strong. Not impressive. Just honest.

Come near. I need You.

In Your name, Amen.

You Did Something Sacred Today

You didn't fail by falling apart. You opened the door by telling the truth. Jesus blesses the poor in spirit—because they're the ones who know they need Him.

And to those who admit the ache... He gives the kingdom.

Tomorrow: Empathy
Today you named the ache. Tomorrow, you'll learn to treat it with kindness—not judgment.

Because you're not broken beyond repair. You're human. And your heart deserves gentleness

Day 2 – *Empathize with Yourself and Others*

Blessed are those who mourn,

for they will be comforted.

—Matthew 5:4—

She stood by the kitchen sink, hands resting on the edge. Dishes clean. Counters wiped. Kids tucked in.

Another ordinary day, but her chest felt tight. Not from anxiety—just a quiet ache she couldn't explain. She wasn't crying. But she could have.

She had no words for the heaviness. Just the familiar urge to push it down, get on with it, and be grateful.

But that ache? It didn't need to be minimized. It needed mercy. And that's exactly what Jesus offers.

Jesus Blesses Grief

Blessed are those who mourn...

Of all the ways Jesus could've continued His most famous sermon, He chose mourning as the next step toward healing.

Not celebration. Not strength. Not spiritual performance.

Mourning.

Grief honors what mattered. It's how the heart says, "This was real. And it mattered."

And Jesus doesn't rush that process—He blesses it. He doesn't say "hurry up and heal." He says, *"you will be comforted."*

Not corrected. Not condemned. *Comforted.*

But while Jesus blesses our grief, most of us have learned to bury it.

Why We Avoid the Pain

Many of us learned that emotion was something to hide, not hold. We were told:

- "Don't cry."
- "Be strong."
- "Keep it together."
- "Choose joy."

And while strength and joy have their place, they were never meant to replace grief. When we don't let sorrow speak, it settles into our bodies. And over time, survival becomes our default—but not our design.

But you were made for more than survival.

You were made to heal. And that starts with permission to feel what you feel—without shame.

To let the tears fall. To name the loss. To say the hard words that live inside your chest.

It's okay to feel the weight of sadness, the sharp edge of grief, the weariness of sorrow. These emotions aren't signs of failure—they're reminders that something mattered enough to mourn.

Honoring them is part of coming back to life. True strength finds its voice in sorrow. And joy doesn't cancel out the need to mourn.

Jesus Wept, Too

At the tomb of Lazarus, Jesus didn't offer a theological explanation. He didn't give a pep talk.

He wept.

He cried over Jerusalem's lostness. He grieved in Gethsemane so deeply He sweat blood. He let sorrow move through Him. Not because He lacked faith, but because He was fully human.

And if Jesus didn't rush His grief, why should you?

You're not being dramatic or faithless. You're being honest. And Jesus is with you in it.

Shared Mourning, Shared Comfort

Grief shrinks in safe company.

Scripture doesn't tell us to cheer people up—it tells us to join them:

Mourn with those who mourn.
—Romans 12:15—

Even Job's friends, for all their flaws, started right.

They sat with him on the ground seven days and
seven nights... for they saw that his
suffering was very great.
—Job 2:13—

You don't have to carry your sorrow alone. And you're not meant to.

Sometimes healing comes through another person simply being present. Sometimes comfort is found in knowing someone else sees your tears and doesn't try to wipe them away too quickly.

Let someone sit with you. Or sit with someone else. That, too, is holy.

Before & After

You're hurting, but you've become a master of disguise. You tell yourself it's not that bad. Others carry heavier burdens. You should be over it by now. So, you push it down. You paste on a smile. You keep your shoulders high and your words strong.

Inside, though, the ache remains—a dull throb beneath the surface. Exhaustion no sleep can fix. Anger that flares too fast. Numbness that creeps in without warning. You survive. But you don't feel whole.

Then something shifts.

You pause.

You let your shoulders drop.

You whisper, *"This hurts."* And for once, you don't chase it away.

You remember Jesus, weeping beside a tomb. His empathy reaches your ache—and slowly, you offer yourself the same. The anger softens. The numbness thaws.

And one day, you sit beside a friend who's hurting—not to fix them, but to be with them. And in that shared silence, something sacred stirs.

Reflection Questions

These aren't questions to perform for. They're invitations to open up and let kindness meet your pain.

- What part of my story have I not allowed myself to grieve?
- Where have I judged myself instead of comforting myself?

- What am I afraid will happen if I stop pretending I'm okay?
- What would it look like to offer this same comfort to someone else this week?

A Breath Prayer

Let your breathing slow. Feel the air enter and leave. Let the words guide you—not just in thought, but in posture.

Inhale: Jesus, You understand...

Exhale: ...And You're with me in this.

Repeat slowly three times. Each breath is a step closer to the God who never leaves.

Healing Practice

1. *Name one loss* you've avoided mourning.

   - A dream that faded
   - A relationship that changed
   - A version of yourself you had to leave behind

2. *Write a short note of compassion* to your past or present self. *"I see the pain you carried in silence. You didn't deserve to walk through that alone."*

3. *Sit in stillness for two minutes.* No fixing. No pressure. Just be present with Jesus.

4. *Speak aloud, even in a whisper: "Mourning is sacred. I am not alone."*

A Closing Prayer

Jesus,

You didn't rush sorrow. You didn't shame the grieving.

You wept. And You're still weeping with us today.

Help me to stop hiding what hurts. Teach me to honor my pain—not as weakness, but as part of being human.

Thank You for never leaving, even when the tears come.

In Your name, Amen.

You've Taken a Gentle Step

Today, you didn't try to power through. You paused. You turned inward with mercy.

You made space for Jesus to meet you—not in the cleaned-up version of your life, but in the part that still hurts.

That's real healing. And it's only just beginning.

Tomorrow: Invite Jesus In

You've named your pain. You've treated it with compassion.

Now, you're ready for the next sacred step:

Opening the door and inviting Jesus into the places you've tried to carry alone.

Because healing doesn't begin with effort. It begins with access.

Day 3 – *Invite Jesus In*

Blessed are the meek,

for they will inherit the earth.

—Matthew 5:5—

He sat at his desk late into the evening, light from the screen painting soft shadows. His work was done, the house quiet—but inside, his heart thudded with a strange ache.

There was a part of him he never spoke about. Not even to God. A regret. A memory. A closed door.

He trusted Jesus with so many things—his prayers, his service, his gratitude. But not *that.*

Until one night, with hands resting in his lap, he whispered, *"Jesus... if You still want in, I'm not hiding anymore. The door's open."*

And that was the beginning.

The Strength of Meekness

Blessed are the meek...

They carry strength the world cannot explain. This isn't weakness—it's unshakable strength wrapped in humility.

Biblical meekness is surrendered strength. It's the kind of strength that listens before it speaks, yields before it conquers, trusts before it controls. Not powerlessness, but power placed gently in God's hands.

Jesus described Himself as "gentle and humble in heart." That's what meekness looks like in a Person—gentle, safe, deeply strong.

When you choose meekness, you're not giving up. You're laying down the illusion that you ever had to carry it all by yourself. You're saying, "I can't do this on my own. And I don't want to anymore."

That's not defeat. That's the doorway to freedom.

Why It Feels Risky to Open the Door

Some of us have had our deepest honesty weaponized. We learned to protect the deepest parts of ourselves—even from God. Control feels safe. Surrender feels scary.

You may think:

- What if He sees what I've been hiding?
- What if I disappoint Him?
- What if I open the door and nothing changes?

But here's what Scripture shows us:

Here I am! I stand at the door and knock. If anyone hears My voice and opens the door, I will come in...
—Revelation 3:20—

Jesus doesn't force His way in. He knocks. He waits. He doesn't push—He pauses until your heart whispers yes.

And when invited—He enters with peace.

Jesus Comes In Gently

In Luke 7, a woman with a wrecked reputation bursts into a dinner party and falls at Jesus' feet. She sobs. She breaks open before Him—no words, just tears.

The others whisper and judge. But Jesus? He sees her. He receives her. And He blesses her surrender with peace.

This is how Jesus responds to brokenness. He doesn't flinch. He doesn't shame. He steps into the sorrow like it's holy ground.

And He will come close to you, too—if you open the door.

Before & After

You move through your days with careful precision. You've built walls that look like resilience. You're strong, independent, capable. You've learned to rely on yourself, to manage your own heart.

Jesus is welcome in many parts of your life—your faith, your service, your gratitude. But that one room? The one where old wounds still ache, where fears still whisper? The door stays shut.

You're afraid of what might happen if you unlock it. Afraid of the mess, the vulnerability, the disappointment. So, you carry the weight alone, believing it's safer that way.

You pause.

You take a deep breath.

And with trembling hands, you reach for the handle.

"Jesus," you whisper, "I don't want to do this alone anymore. Come in."

It's not a polished prayer. Just honesty. A crack in the wall of self-reliance. And something shifts. His presence settles gently around you—not rushing, not fixing, but simply there.

You begin to show Him the contents of that space—the pain, the fear, the buried memories. You hold out what you once hid. And He doesn't turn away. And you realize: He is kind. He is steady. And your softness isn't weakness—it's sacred.

You don't feel the same. *You feel held.*

Reflection Questions

- What part of my heart have I tried to carry without Jesus?

- Where am I still clinging to control because surrender feels risky?
- What's one way I could make space for Jesus in the part I've kept hidden?

To invite Him in might begin with a simple whisper: *"Jesus, I need You here."* It might involve unlocking the door to a memory long avoided. Or it might mean creating space in silence, trusting that He's present even when unseen.

A Breath Prayer

Let your body relax. Breathe slowly. Let this prayer soften your edges. Let it carry you toward surrender.

Inhale: Jesus, I trust You...

Exhale: ...Come into this place.

Repeat slowly three times. Let each breath be an open door.

Healing Practice

1. *Name the place you've kept closed.*
    - A wound from childhood
    - A private struggle
    - A fear that still feels too big

2. *Write a short prayer of invitation. "Jesus, I've guarded this part of me. But I don't want to carry it alone anymore. I welcome You in."*

3. *Sit in stillness for two minutes.*

    - Let your breath settle. You don't have to understand it all—just let Him near.

    - Picture Jesus gently entering that space.

    - Not to fix it on the spot, but simply to be with you in it.

4. *Whisper aloud: "I don't have to carry this alone anymore."*

A Closing Prayer

Jesus,

I've locked the door long enough.

I've carried this by myself.

Today, I open the door. Not because I'm brave.

Just because I need You.

Come into every room of my soul. And stay.

In Your name, Amen.

You Took a Holy Step Today

You didn't try to fix everything. You didn't have to clean the whole house. You just opened one door. And heaven noticed.

Jesus meets you there—with no rush, no pressure, just presence.

This is meekness: strength handed over. It's the courage to stop carrying what you were never meant to. And this is where the healing deepens.

Tomorrow: Own What's Yours

Now that Jesus is in the room, it's time to take the next step—one that many avoid, but few regret:

Owning your part in the pain, the patterns, or the process. Not with guilt. But with courage.

Because the moment you own what's yours... God begins to transform it.

✣

You're healing in ways you can't yet see. —Jesus

Day 4 – *Own What's Yours*

Blessed are those who hunger and thirst
for righteousness, for they will be filled.
—Matthew 5:6—

She stood in the doorway of her living room, clutching a coffee mug she'd reheated three times. Kids were arguing in the next room. Her chest felt tight—not from the noise, but from the same emotional loop spinning again.

The same script. The same cycle. The same silent ache. She closed her eyes and whispered, *"Lord, I don't want to stay stuck."*

And that whisper became the sacred shift.

You Can't Heal What You Won't Own

There's a sacred moment in every healing journey, isn't there?

It's the pivot. The moment from pain-awareness to Spirit-led ownership.

It's the moment you stop saying, *"I guess this is just how I'll always be,"* and start whispering, *"I believe there's more than this—and with God's help, I'm moving toward it."*

Maybe it's a habit you've justified too long. A wound you've protected so fiercely it became part of your identity. A pattern you've repeated—not because you're bad, but because you've been stuck.

You didn't cause all the pain. But with Christ, you're ready now—no more circling. No more rehearsing the pain. No more looking back for permission to move forward. You've circled this mountain long enough—and now you're ready to step forward.

It's time to step out—and let grace catch you.

That's where real healing ignites.

When We Reach for Blame

When we're hurting, it's almost instinct, isn't it? To reach for reasons outside ourselves:

- "They made me feel this way."
- "That situation wrecked me."
- "If life had been different, I wouldn't be like this."

And maybe there's truth in those statements. Maybe there's validity in the pain.

But healing doesn't wait for the world to rearrange itself. It begins in that Spirit-anchored moment—when you pause...take a holy breath, "Jesus, I'm willing to look at what's mine to carry—and surrender it to You."

That's not blame. That's breakthrough.

What It Means to Hunger for Righteousness

Righteousness... it's not about rigid performance, is it? This journey doesn't require perfection—it invites truth.

In Scripture, righteousness means alignment—living in right relationship:

- With God, first and foremost.
- With others, in honesty and love.
- With yourself, in self-compassion and grace.

So, when we hunger and thirst for righteousness—when we long to live in the flow of God's goodness—it's like a dislocated joint finding its place again. There's a deep ache until alignment comes—and when it does, everything moves more freely.

And Jesus doesn't meet that hunger with guilt. He meets it with fullness.

Why Ownership Feels Risky

Let's be honest...we'd often rather numb the pain, explain it away, or delay the confrontation than take responsibility for our part.

It's hard to whisper, *"I've been reacting out of fear."* Or, *"I've been repeating the same story to protect myself."* Or even, *"I've been believing a lie about who I am."*

But confession isn't punishment. It's release.

If we confess our sins, He is faithful and just to forgive us our sins and to cleanse us...
—1 John 1:9—

When we name what's broken within, we don't receive shame—we receive grace.

When You Bring It, Jesus Fills It

Think of Zacchaeus in Luke 19.

He climbed a tree, desperate just to glimpse Jesus. But what changed everything? His ownership.

He declared, *"I've wronged people. I'll make it right."*

And Jesus responded:

Today salvation has come to this house... for the Son of Man came to seek and to save the lost.
—Luke 19:9-10—

Jesus didn't shame Zacchaeus—He celebrated the turning point. And when you name your truth and turn toward healing, He'll meet you the same way: with joy, not judgment.

Before & After

You navigate your days with a sense of resignation. Things happen to you. People trigger you. Circumstances dictate your mood. You're a leaf blown by the wind.

You explain. You deflect. Always 'because of' something else.

You feel stuck, powerless, ashamed. You long for change, but don't know how to begin.

You pause.

You take a deep breath.

You begin to sift through the story.

You ask, gently: *"Okay, what's mine in this?" "What am I responsible for?"*

This isn't punishment. It's the start of clarity and grace. It's Christ-centered ownership. You realize you're not a leaf. You're a tree—rooted, able to grow.

You start to own your reactions, your patterns, your choices. You confess where you've missed the mark.

And in that naming, you find new strength. You're not a victim anymore. You're part of the healing—with Jesus at your side.

Reflection Questions

- What pattern or reaction have I justified instead of owning?
- What belief about myself is keeping me stuck in this cycle?
- What would it look like to take responsibility—with Jesus, not apart from Him?

Ownership sounds like this: *"My reaction came from fear—not faith."*

It trades blame for honesty. It's not weakness—it's strength, anchored in grace.

It's the courage to say, *"I'm not finished yet. But grace still meets me here."*

A Breath Prayer

Let your breath slow. Let this become your posture.

Inhale: God, I want to be whole...

Exhale: ...Help me see what's mine to own—and what's not.

Repeat slowly three times. This isn't self-criticism—it's sacred courage.

Healing Practice

1. *Ask the Holy Spirit* to gently reveal one area where you've been protecting, deflecting, or denying.

2. *Write a simple, honest prayer: "Jesus, I've been reacting out of— / hiding behind— / believing lies like—I bring it all into Your light. I want to live free—free with You, not apart from You."*

3. *Sit in stillness for two minutes.*

    - Don't rush to fix it.

    - Just let Jesus stand with you in it—steady and kind.

4. *Say aloud: "I'm not afraid to own this. Grace already has—and Jesus isn't going anywhere."*

Live It Out

What reaction, wound, or belief is yours to own—and Jesus's to heal?

Take one small step today. Share it with a friend. Or write it down as a sacred marker.

Jesus will meet you in the movement.

You Took a Brave Step Today

Today wasn't about piling on guilt. It was about gaining clarity.

You named your part. You brought it into the light. You said yes to alignment and no to shame.

This is what it means to hunger and thirst for righteousness. And Jesus promised: *you will be filled.*

A Closing Prayer

Jesus,

I've blamed, deflected, and stayed stuck in cycles I don't want anymore.

But today I see it: part of this is mine to own.

Not so I carry it forever—but so I can finally surrender it to You.

Help me stand in truth, not shame. And as I bring it to You, remind me again: grace meets me here.

In Your name, Amen.

Tomorrow: Extend Mercy

You've named the pain. You've owned your part.

Now it's time for the next, equally vital step: releasing what others have done to you.

Forgiveness isn't approval. It's not pretending it didn't hurt. It's releasing the weight—even if they never apologize.

It's freedom. And you're ready for it.

Day 5 – *Understand the Story Behind the Struggle*

Blessed are the merciful,

for they will be shown mercy.

—Matthew 5:7—

He left the lunch table more rattled than he let on. One offhand comment from a friend and—snap. Not loud—just curt, cold, quick.

Later in his car, replaying it, his chest tightened. *"Why did that hit so hard?"*

And then it surfaced.

It wasn't really about the friend. It was the echo of a father's voice—sharp words that didn't shape, but scraped. He hadn't noticed how close they still lived beneath the surface.

He didn't beat himself up. Not this time.

He whispered instead: *"Jesus, I think I'm ready to look at this with You."*

The Strongest Reactions Come From The Deepest Places

When emotions flare or thoughts spiral, we tend to shut down, don't we? Or we beat ourselves up, replaying the moment, dissecting our failure.

We think:

- *Why am I still like this?*
- *I should be past this by now.*
- *Something must be fundamentally wrong with me.*

But these reactions aren't random. They're not character flaws or spiritual deficiencies.

They're echoes of moments we've buried, minimized, or forgotten. Old pain still echoes in us.

You're not broken. You're carrying a story.

And the strongest parts of you?

They're the ones that walked through fire—and didn't shut down.

They survived.

Now they're ready to heal.

Now it's time to understand that story—not just outlast it.

Mercy Begins With Insight

Blessed are the merciful...

And sometimes, the first person who needs that mercy—is you.

Mercy begins when judgment gives way to understanding—not to excuse, but to reveal what's still unhealed.

For we do not have a high priest who is unable
to empathize with our weaknesses...
—Hebrews 4:15—

Jesus doesn't diagnose from a distance—He draws near and stays.

Mercy blossoms when you start listening to your pain instead of scolding it.

Signs You're Still Holding the Gavel

- You call yourself names no one else does.
- You feel guilty for emotions that don't make sense.
- You "should" yourself more than you comfort yourself.
- You replay failures long after everyone else has moved on.
- You expect more compassion from Jesus than you give to yourself.

Friend, you've held the gavel long enough. It's time to set it down—and let mercy take the bench.

Why We Avoid The Deeper Story

We protect what we don't want to feel. So, we push through. Stay busy. Stay distracted.

But Jesus doesn't bring things up to shame you. He surfaces them to walk you through.

And He'll walk at your pace.

No force. No rush.

Just mercy—steady and sure.

On The Road To Emmaus

Two disciples walked away from Jerusalem, didn't they?

Confused. Disappointed. Their hearts cracked with grief.

Jesus joined them, unrecognized. He asked, *"What are you discussing?"*

They poured it out: *"We had hoped He was the one..."*

He listened. He walked with them. And when the silence had done its work, He opened their eyes.

This is how Jesus walks with you, too:

Not with impatience. But with insight. Not with shame. But with understanding.

Discernment vs. Judgment

There's a difference, you know.

Judgment slams the door. Discernment knocks and waits.

Judgment says, 'You're the problem.'

Discernment says, 'Let's be curious. Let's look at this together—with Jesus.

Discernment asks better questions. And mercy listens for the answer.

It's where healing begins.

Before & After

You're triggered again. But it's not just the words—it's how fast your chest tightens, how sharp your response feels, even to you.

You tell yourself it's their fault. Their tone. Their timing. Their insensitivity.

You walk away frustrated, not just with them—but with yourself.

The reaction came fast. Too fast.

And afterward, that quiet question stirs again: "Why do I always do this?"

You slow down.

Not all at once—but enough to breathe, enough to ask, "What's underneath that reaction?"

This time, you don't shame yourself. You trace the flare-up back to something older—a wound that never got language, just silence.

You don't run. You let Jesus meet you there.

You don't try to fix it. You listen. You stay.

And for the first time, your heart doesn't feel like the enemy. It feels like a story.

Not fully healed. But finally heard.

Reflection Questions

- What recent situation stirred more emotion than the moment called for?
- What memory, belief, or old fear might be connected to that reaction?
- Where do I need Jesus to help me understand—not just react?

Pay attention to the echoes—they often carry the real story. Triggered responses often come from old wounds.

A Breath Prayer

Let the words carry you gently—not with pressure, but permission.

Inhale: Jesus, show me what's true...

Exhale: even if it hurts a little.

Repeat slowly. Be curious, not critical.

Healing Practice

1. *Name one pattern* that keeps surfacing—anger, fear, defensiveness, control, whatever it is.
2. *Ask:* When did I first feel this? Let the Holy Spirit bring a moment to mind. Don't force it—just notice.
3. *Picture Jesus* entering that memory with you. Let Him be present—not to fix it instantly, but to comfort.
4. *Ask Him:* What do You want me to know about this moment?
5. *Write two truths:*
    - What I believed then
    - What I believe now
6. Let Jesus be the Author now—helping you rewrite the story. Then say aloud:

"I see what I couldn't see before. I name it now, not with shame, but with truth. I receive Your mercy—right here, where it first hurt... and where healing begins."

A Closing Prayer

Jesus,

I see it now. The moment it began.

You're there—not to scold, but to hold.

Teach me how to carry this story—not as a wound to hide, but as a place where grace walked in.

In Your name, Amen.

You Took A Brave Step Today

You didn't just feel—you followed the feeling back to its roots. You let Jesus walk into something older, something deeper.

And there? You didn't find judgment. You found mercy.

This is how healing unfolds: Not in force, but in revelation. Not all at once—but one memory, one insight, one moment of mercy at a time.

Tomorrow: Yield To Healing

Now that you've begun to see what's been buried, the next step is letting go. You don't have to fix it all. You don't have to hold it all.

Tomorrow, we'll step into surrender.

Because healing deepens when you stop trying to carry it alone—and let Jesus carry you.

❖

Don't measure your healing. Just stay close to Me. —Jesus

Day 6 – *Yield to Healing*

Blessed are the pure in heart,
for they will see God.
—Matthew 5:8—

I used to think healing was a battle I had to win, didn't you?

If I just prayed with enough fervor. If I sacrificed enough comfort. If I examined every crack and crevice of my soul—patched each one with spiritual duct tape, pressure, and perfectionism.

Then, *finally*, I'd earn my peace.

But healing doesn't spring from pressure, does it? It doesn't bow to our striving.

Healing comes from presence. And presence? It begins with surrender.

When Letting Go Feels Like Giving Up

Maybe you've done everything you know how to do. You've prayed the prayers. You've shown up at church. You've diligently worked through all the steps.

And still... something feels stubbornly stuck.

That doesn't mean you've failed, you know. It doesn't mean you're destined to stay in this place. It simply means you've arrived at the very spot where healing *often* begins: *release.*

Yielding is like finally unclenching a fist you didn't even realize you'd been holding tight. You're not losing anything by opening your hand—just the tightness, the white-knuckle grip, the weight of trying to hold everything together on your own.

Many, many people feel this way, but don't dare speak it aloud. You're not alone in your weariness. You're not the only one tired of white-knuckling your way through life.

Striving shouts, "Push harder!"

Yielding whispers, You're safe now. Let go.

The Lord is your Shepherd—you don't have to carry this alone.

Healing isn't something you force. It's something you receive.

What It Means To Be Pure In Heart

Jesus said the pure in heart would see God. Not the perfect ones, mind you. Not the ones who've conquered every flaw and mastered every emotion.

The pure in heart—those who are undivided, unclenched, willing. A pure heart doesn't try to both trust and control at the very same time, does it? It simply says, *"God, I'm giving this back to You. It's Yours now."*

Yielding is giving God access to what you're utterly exhausted of carrying. And when you yield, something *does* begin to shift, doesn't it?

When the deafening noise of control finally quiets down, the vision of who God truly is starts to sharpen, to return.

Why Surrender Feels Risky

Surrender doesn't often feel like sweet peace at the outset, does it? It often feels like stepping off a cliff, like losing your footing and plummeting into the unknown.

We've learned to survive, haven't we, by gripping tightly, by holding it all together with Herculean effort.

Control felt like safety. But it kept us from receiving real comfort.

Real rest.

Surrender feels scary, doesn't it, because it means we're no longer in the driver's seat, calling all the shots. But it's also the very place where grace becomes undeniably, beautifully *real.*

You're not giving up. You're giving it back—to the One who can actually carry it.

Jesus In The Garden

No one modeled surrender with more raw honesty than Jesus Himself, did they? In Gethsemane, He wasn't hiding His anguish, His turmoil. He let it all surface.

"If there's any other way..."

And then, the ultimate yielding—*"Not My will, but Yours."*

Even Jesus, sweating drops of blood in His sorrow, pleaded for a different path before surrendering fully to the Father's.

Jesus didn't surrender because He had no choice.

He surrendered because He fully trusted the Father—even in the dark, even through the tears.

Before & After

You're tired, aren't you? Bone-tired. Soul-tired. You've been pushing, striving, *trying* so hard to make it all work, to manufacture your own healing.

You're tightly wound, aren't you? Every muscle clenched, every nerve on high alert. You're determined to control the outcome, to steer the ship, to ensure it doesn't sink.

You pray, but your prayers feel strained, forced. You serve, but your service feels joyless, dutiful.

You're afraid, aren't you, that if you loosen your grip, everything will fall apart.

You slow down, don't you?

You exhale deeply.

You allow your body to soften, to relax its defenses.

"God," you whisper, "I'm done trying to run the show. I'm giving You the wheel... and I choose to keep showing up to the work that heals me."

It's a shaky surrender. A fragile, trembling release. But it's the kind of beginning God always notices.

Because in that yielding, you don't collapse—you unfold.

You discover a quiet kind of space—one you forgot you needed. A place to breathe.

Permission to be—without striving to prove.

You realize something you never dared believe: you're not falling.

You're being held. Not in weakness—but in love. And you're not just letting go of control—you're reaching for wholeness. You're making choices that honor your well-being.

You're walking your healing journey with God, not just in His direction, but right beside Him.

Reflection Questions

- What part of my healing am I still trying to manage, to control?
- What am I most afraid would happen if I fully let go and surrendered?

- What would it feel like, in your body, in your soul, to stop striving and start truly trusting?

To yield is to exchange the burden of control for the lightness of trust. It's to trade the illusion of self-reliance for the reality of His sustaining presence. It's to open our hands, not knowing what will come, but believing it will be good.

A Breath Prayer

Slow your breath. Let your body rest.

Inhale: Jesus, I let go...

Exhale: ...so You can heal me.

Repeat gently. Three times is often enough. Or more, if you need it.

Healing Practice

1. Identify one specific place where you've been striving—emotionally, spiritually, relationally, whatever comes to mind.
2. Write a surrender prayer, from your heart to His: "Jesus, I've carried this for far too long. I yield it completely to You. I give You full access."
3. Sit in stillness for two full minutes. If silence feels uncomfortable, gently repeat: "You are my Healer, and I trust You in this space."

4. If it feels right, open your hands, palms up, as a physical sign of release, of letting go.

5. Place your hand over your heart and whisper, with whatever courage you can offer: "This space, this burden, this part of me, belongs to You now."

You Entered Sacred Ground Today

Today, you didn't give up, did you? You gave God room. Room to move, room to work, room to do what only He can.

You stopped striving—and started softening. You chose to trust. You released the illusion of control—and tentatively, you took hold of a deeper peace.

This is what it means, isn't it, to be pure in heart.

Not flawless. Not perfect. But surrendered.

And Jesus promised: you *will* see God.

Tomorrow: Become A Peacemaker

Now that you've yielded, you're ready to carry something profoundly new, aren't you?

Peace.

Not a fragile peace that crumbles when life gets hard—but one that flows from walking with the Healer.

Tomorrow, we'll explore what it means to become a refuge, a haven of that peace, for others.

Because healing isn't just something we receive. It's something we're called to carry, to extend, to offer to a world desperately in need.

Day 7 – *Carry Peace*

Blessed are the peacemakers,
for they will be called children of God.
—Matthew 5:9—

I used to think being a peacemaker meant one thing, didn't you?

Staying quiet. Keeping the waters calm. Never, ever rocking the boat.

But peace doesn't spring from silence, does it? It's not the absence of conflict—it's the presence of something deeper.

Peacemakers aren't the ones who've somehow escaped struggle, are they?

They're the ones who choose to show up, even in the mess, carrying something far deeper than control—a peace that's been forged in the fires of surrender.

What Peace Really Looks Like

Peace often tiptoes in quietly, doesn't it? It's not usually loud or flashy. But that doesn't equate to weakness—not in the slightest.

- It's the friend who truly listens without trying to fix.

- It's the parent who stays steady in the middle of chaos.
- It's the person who walks into a tense room and brings kindness, not fear.

You don't become a peacemaker by fixing others—but by carrying the peace God formed in you.

And that peace doesn't stop with you. It flows through you—like a candle lighting another.

Quiet, yes. But powerful. Ongoing. Holy.

Peace Flows From Surrender

Peace isn't a personality trait. It's not a skillset or something you fake your way into. It's something that grows when you stop striving and let mercy take root.

But the fruit of the Spirit is love, joy, peace...
—Galatians 5:22—

Peace is the fruit of a surrendered heart. It grows in the soil of mercy, healing, and trust.

What you've received... was never meant to stay bottled up. It's meant to be poured out, shared, and carried forward.

Peace doesn't mean silence—it means presence.

Why We Pull Back From Peacemaking

Some of us hesitate, don't we? We've confused peacemaking with passivity. Or we've been burned by conflict and now fear being misunderstood.

But peacemaking isn't people-pleasing. And it's not about sacrificing your well-being for someone else's comfort. It's about presence.

If it is possible, as far as it depends on you, live
at peace with everyone.
—Romans 12:18—

You're not responsible for how others respond. You're only responsible for what you carry in.

Jesus, the First Peacemaker

When Jesus walked into that locked room after the resurrection, His first words weren't a rebuke.

Not a lecture. Not an "I told you so." They were: "Peace be with you."

He brought calm where there had been paralyzing fear. He offered forgiveness where there had been devastating failure.

He didn't demand immediate change. He delivered the very essence of peace. And now, He invites you to become what He was—to carry calm where there's chaos, grace where there's grief, and peace where fear has settled in.

When you walk into a room, you're not merely arriving—you're representing Him. You are carrying peace.

And that peace, beloved, has a name: *child of God.*

You don't have to force peace—you just have to carry it.

Before & After

You've learned to avoid conflict. You smooth things over, change the subject, keep the peace—at least on the surface.

But inside? You're anxious. Drained. Tense. You long for connection, but you're afraid honesty might break the illusion of calm.

You step into hard spaces with a stillness inside.

You're not there to fix or control—you're there to carry peace.

You listen.

You speak with grace. You're not afraid of the mess.

You've become a safe harbor, a calm presence in a storm. And you've discovered that the very peace God gave you was always meant to be given away.

Reflection Questions

- Where have I experienced God's peace most clearly in this healing journey?
- Who in my life needs peace—not solutions, just presence?
- What would it look like to live as a peacemaker this week in small, practical ways?

To make peace is to become a bridge, not a barrier. To extend understanding instead of accusation. Grace instead of judgment. You're simply giving what you've received.

A Breath Prayer

Let this mark not just the end of a day, but the beginning of a new rhythm.

Inhale: Jesus, make me a vessel...

Exhale: ...who carries Your peace into every room.

Repeat slowly three times. Let it settle in your soul.

Healing Practice

1. *Think of one situation or relationship* that's crying out for peace.
2. *Invite Jesus* to fill you, to saturate you with His Spirit.

3. Write this declaration in your journal or whisper it aloud: *"I am a peacemaker—not because I have all the answers, but because I've been formed, and I've been filled."*

4. *Take one gentle step* toward peace: a kind message, a listening ear, a soft word.

5. *Optional: Light a candle or simply sit quietly with God.* Whisper this blessing aloud. Let it land like truth. **"Peace lives in me now. I carry what God has healed."**

6. Say it again tomorrow.

7. And again the next day—until it starts to feel like the truth.

You've Come Full Circle

(But You're Just Getting Started)

Seven days ago, you admitted the ache. Now, you've become a wellspring.

You welcomed Jesus in. Surrendered control. Received mercy. Heard the truth.

You've stopped striving and started yielding. You are not the same person who began this journey.

You are a peacemaker.

Not because you've arrived—but because God has worked. And the world needs what you now carry.

Commissioning Prayer

Jesus,

You placed peace in me—gentle, steady, hard-won.

Now lead me to the places, the relationships, the hearts where that peace can take root and begin to heal.

Let my presence become soil—soft enough for others to believe again.

In Your name, Amen.

Now go—carry that peace into a world desperate for it.

❖

Before we move on, I want to slow the pace a little.

The next section isn't just more teaching—it's a personal map.

These "Vicious Cycles" describe what stuck feels like, and how Jesus meets us there. If you've been wondering, *"What does healing look like for me?"*—this is where things get practical.

❖

"Let it sink in. You're not the same as when you began."

Part 3

Defeating the Cycles That Keep Us Stuck

These next pages aren't extras. They're part of your healing.

They're a mirror—revealing the patterns that keep us stuck, and the grace that helps us break free.

Search me, God, and know my heart. —Psalms 139:23

These twelve cycles tend to surface in different ways, across different seasons. You'll likely see yourself in one—or more.

Don't rush this part. Ask the Holy Spirit to shine a gentle light on the cycle still whispering in your life.

This *is* your healing. If one cycle feels loud, start there.

I've seen it all. And I'm still here. —Jesus

Chapter 4
ANGER ARMOR
When hurt gets armored instead of healed

Anger Armor is what we build when we've been hurt. You protect yourself because you've been hurt—but armor keeps love out, too. It starts with a wound—real, sharp, personal. But instead of grieving or healing, we reach for protection.

Anger becomes the cover. And over time, that anger hardens into armor. It keeps more pain out, yes—but it also keeps people out. Even God can feel distant when you're armored up.

How It Starts to Spiral

It starts with a *Wound.* Maybe someone betrayed you. Maybe life hit hard—suddenly, unfairly. Maybe you've been carrying pain so long you forgot how it started. But the hurt is real—and unresolved.

Then comes *Blame.* We direct our pain outward. "If they hadn't..." or "It's their fault I'm like this." Blame feels like control, but it keeps us locked in the pain.

So we *Push Away.* People get too close, we back up. Emotions rise, we shut down. Even with those we love most, we create distance—just in case they hurt us too.

And finally, we *Build Walls.* Not physical ones, but emotional barriers. We don't say what we feel. We don't let others in. And slowly, the person inside the armor becomes someone no one really knows—sometimes not even you.

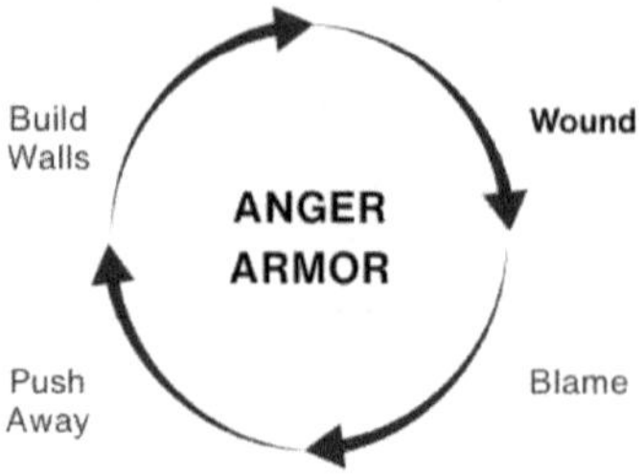

Round and round it goes. Every new wound confirms why you need to stay guarded. Every wall gets taller. Every push away feels like survival. But you're not surviving—you're suffocating.

What's Still True About You

You don't have to stay in this armor.

The anger was never your enemy—it just wasn't meant to stay. Scripture doesn't avoid anger. It meets us there. It says *"Be angry, and do not sin."* (Ephesians 4:26). God understands your anger. He just doesn't want it to rule you.

"Refrain from anger and turn from wrath; do not fret—it leads only to evil." (Psalm 37:8) Anger, when held too long, becomes a poison. Not to the one who hurt you—but to you.

But here's the good news: *"He heals the brokenhearted and binds up their wounds."* (Psalm 147:3) The wound isn't the end of the story.

You don't have to guard it forever. You can bring it to God—raw, aching, unedited.

What's true is this: You were hurt. But you are not just your hurt. You were wounded. But you are not just your wound. You're more than the bruise. You're the beloved underneath it.

And you don't have to carry it alone anymore.

Someone Just Like You

There's a woman in Scripture who knew this cycle well. Her name's not recorded, but her pain is. She came to Jesus with a jar of perfume and a heart full of grief (Luke 7). She'd lived a life marked by shame, anger, and being pushed aside.

But that night, she knelt at His feet. She didn't argue. She didn't explain. She didn't hide behind armor. She wept.

And Jesus saw her—not just her pain, but her. He saw the longing behind her tears, the faith behind her silence, the story behind her shame. Then He said, *"Your faith has saved you. Go in peace."*

She walked away freer than she'd ever been.

The Way Out Begins Here

Take a breath. Close your eyes. Let this truth settle over your heart:

You can put the armor down. You've worn steel long enough—let the soft hands of grace undo the buckles.

Not all at once. Maybe not today. But you can begin.

- *Start by grieving instead of blaming*
- *Let love in instead of pushing people away.*
- *Open your hands—one wall at a time.*

God is not angry at your anger. But He's ready to lead you through it—toward healing, not hiding.

You don't have to protect yourself anymore. You're already protected in Him.

I've worn this armor too. It's heavy. And healing, friend, is lighter than hiding.

Try These Prayers

Anger often shows up as protection—but underneath it is pain. You don't have to pretend it's not there. You don't have to manage it alone. Let this be a moment to loosen your grip and let God hold what's underneath.

A Prayer of Release

God,

You see what's behind this anger. You know what hurt me.

I've tried to cover the pain. I've tried to guard my heart on my own.

But the armor is heavy.

Today, I lay one piece down.

I trust You to hold what I've carried.

I trust You to heal what I've hidden—even from myself.

I trust You to be my defender.

In Jesus' name, Amen.

A Breath Prayer

Inhale: You see my pain...

Exhale: ...You carry my healing.

Let this breath become your rhythm. One release at a time. You don't have to take the armor off all at once—just enough to breathe again.

Where the Armor Cracks Open

You're not too broken to heal. You're not too angry to be seen, to be known, to be loved. You're not too guarded to be found.

This loop—this Anger Armor—doesn't have to define your days. It was never meant to. The walls can come down. And what's waiting on the other side isn't more pain—it's peace.

Take the first step.

Jesus is already waiting on the other side.

When armor rusts, it weakens. When hearts soften, they heal.

Chapter 5

THE PEOPLE-PLEASING LOOP

When being liked costs more than being whole

People-Pleasing often starts as something good—kindness, care, compassion. But somewhere along the way, it becomes something else. You begin to say yes even when you mean no. You carry their expectations like a backpack full of bricks. You avoid conflict. You edit yourself. You smile when you're breaking inside.

You protect peace by silencing your voice—and slowly losing your soul. It feels safer that way—until it doesn't.

People-pleasing seems like love. But it's often fear dressed in kindness.

How It Starts to Spiral

It begins with a *Need to Be Liked.* Deep down, you crave connection. You long to be seen and accepted. So you do what seems safe: you make yourself agreeable. You serve. You avoid rocking the boat.

Then you start *Saying Yes Too Much.* Not just to tasks or favors—but to roles you were never meant to carry. You take care of everyone else, while quietly neglecting your own needs. Your boundaries blur. Your soul stretches thin.

Eventually, you *Feel Used.* But instead of speaking up, you wonder if it's your fault. You think, *"Maybe I'm not doing enough. Maybe I need to try harder."* So you keep going, even when you're empty.

And then comes the loop-closing trap: *Fear of Rejection.* The thought of disappointing someone paralyzes you. So you say yes again. And the cycle resets.

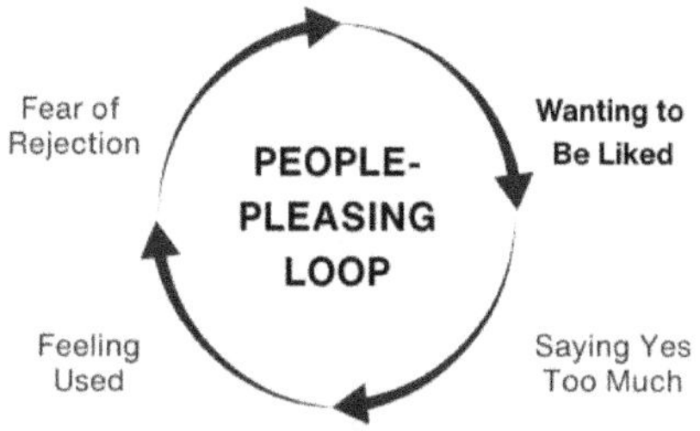

It looks like loyalty. But it feels like resentment. And underneath it all, you're afraid of who might leave if you finally speak the truth.

What's Still True About You

You don't have to prove your worth to be loved.

God didn't create you to live at the mercy of other people's moods. You're not responsible for managing everyone else's feelings. You are allowed to have a voice. You are allowed to say no.

Scripture reminds us: *"Fear of man will prove to be a snare, but whoever trusts in the Lord is kept safe."* (Proverbs 29:25)

Trying to please everyone will always cost too much. It's exhausting. But trusting God with your identity? That's where safety lives.

Paul said it this way: *"Am I now trying to win the approval of human beings, or of God?"* (Galatians 1:10)

What's true is this: You are already loved. Already chosen. Already known. You don't need their yes to rest in God's yes.

Someone Just Like You

Martha was a helper. A doer. A good hostess. But when Jesus came to her home, she got swept up in the serving and missed the moment (Luke 10).

Her sister Mary sat at Jesus' feet. But Martha felt pressure—the kind that comes when you believe your value is tied to your usefulness.

She said to Jesus, *"Don't you care that my sister has left me to do the work by myself?"* (Luke 10:40)

Jesus loved Martha. He wasn't mad at her. But He gently told her the truth: *"You are worried and upset about many things, but only one thing is needed."*

Martha wasn't wrong. She was just worn out. Caught in a loop. And Jesus invited her out of it—not by doing more, but by choosing better.

The Way Out Begins Here

You can stop performing.

You can say no without guilt. You can rest without explanation. You can disappoint someone and still be deeply loved by God.

Start here:

- *Say yes when it's true.*
- *Say no when it sets you free.*
- *Say nothing when silence is strength—not fear.*

You're not here to earn a spot at the table. Jesus already pulled out a chair.

You're not here to keep everyone happy. You're here to walk in truth, with grace.

Lay the pressure down. Pick up peace instead.

Try These Prayers

Let's take a moment to breathe and be honest. This loop often hides behind good intentions—but it leaves your soul tired. So let's not fix it. Let's pray through it.

A Prayer of Surrender:

God,

You know how tired I am of trying to keep everyone happy.

I've said yes too much and lost myself in the process.

I've tried to earn love You already gave me for free.

Today, I want to let that go.

Teach me how to speak with courage and rest in grace.

Help me trust that the only approval I need is Yours.

In Jesus' name, Amen.

A Breath Prayer:

Inhale: I am already loved...

Exhale: ...I don't have to prove it.

Let this prayer be the start of something honest. You don't have to pretend anymore. God sees you. Loves you. Chooses you—even when you're still learning to choose yourself.

Where the Loop Starts to Break

You are not too much—and you don't have to become less to be loved.

This loop—this People-Pleasing—doesn't have to run your life anymore. You can say no. You can be whole. You can be honest.

And the ones who truly love you? They'll still be there.

Take the first step. *Jesus already said yes to you.*

Chapter 6

THE GUILT LOOP

When effort replaces grace, you just feel worse

Guilt has a way of sounding holy—but it wears you out.

You mess up. Or maybe you just feel off. And suddenly, there's a weight on your chest and a script in your head: *Try harder. Do more. Make it right.*

You apologize again. You overcompensate. You pray longer. You serve more. And underneath it all is this ache: *"Have I done enough?"*

You carry the pressure to make things right—even when grace already did. You protect yourself with performance. But it doesn't heal the ache.

This isn't conviction—it's captivity. Jesus didn't bring heavier chains. He came to break them.

How It Starts to Spiral

This loop doesn't announce itself with fanfare. It creeps in—quiet, convincing, exhausting. Here's how it often unfolds:

1. *You miss the mark.* A mistake. A failure. A moment you wish you could undo.

2. *You turn inward.* Self-blame kicks in. You replay it, picking apart every word, every look.

3. *You strive to make up for it.* You serve harder, pray longer, do more—hoping to earn back what grace already gave.

4. *You burn out.* You run out of energy but not out of shame. And that convinces you you've failed again.

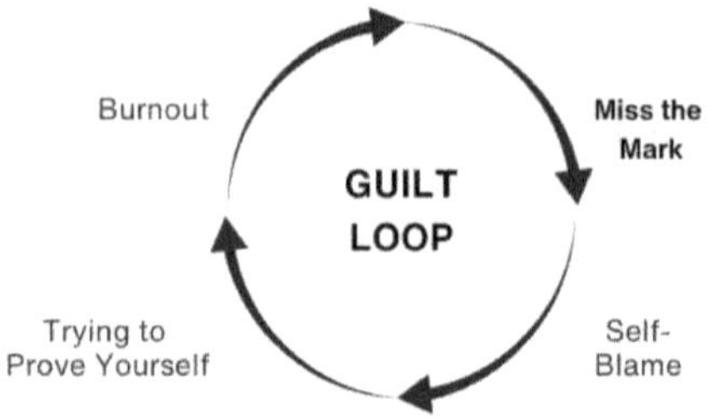

Guilt keeps you circling—always reaching, never resting.

What's Still True About You

You are not your lowest moment. And you don't have to prove your worth to God.

The Bible says, *"There is now no condemnation for those who are in Christ Jesus."* (Romans 8:1)

That means the voice of guilt doesn't get the last word. Grace isn't earned. It was always a gift.

You don't clean yourself up before coming to God. You come as you are—and He meets you there, arms already open—no scolding, no delay.

You are already forgiven. Already welcomed. Already held.

That's the truth. Let it be louder than the guilt.

Someone Just Like You

Peter knows the loop you're in. He swore he'd never abandon Jesus. But fear won. And when the pressure hit, he denied even knowing Him—three times (Luke 22).

Then the rooster crowed. Peter fell apart. Shame collapsed him before he could even speak.

He wept bitterly, soaked in regret. But Jesus didn't write him off.

After the resurrection, Jesus made him breakfast on the beach. He didn't demand an apology. He asked a question: *"Do you love Me?"* (John 21)

Three denials. Three affirmations. And then a mission: *"Feed My sheep."*

Jesus didn't just forgive Peter—He re-called him.

That's what grace does. It doesn't just restore—it re-calls.

The Way Out Begins Here

If you're stuck in the guilt loop, this may feel impossible. But the truth is: you get to trust your way out—not try.

Here's where the break begins:

- *Lay down the replay loop.* You don't have to keep revisiting what's already been forgiven.
- *Lay down the pressure to fix what's already been forgiven.* God isn't asking you to earn your place back.
- *Lay down the voice that says you're disqualified.* The cross already covered it.

These aren't performance steps. They're soul-level surrenders—each one loosening guilt's grip a little more.

Try These Prayers

When guilt clings close, grace often feels distant. But God isn't far. He's right here. Let these prayers help you name what's heavy—and let it go.

A Breath Prayer

Inhale: I am fully forgiven...

Exhale: ...I don't have to earn it.

A Prayer of Release

Jesus,

I keep trying to carry what You already carried for me.

I confess the guilt that follows me and the pressure I feel to make it right.

But You never asked me to fix myself.

You just asked me to come.

So here I am.

I let go of guilt.

I open my hands to grace.

Wash me. Steady me again. Carry me home..

In Your name, Amen.

Let this be the moment you quit rehearsing regret—and start receiving redemption.

Where the Loop Starts to Break

You are not too stained to be clean. You are not too broken to be made whole. You are not too far gone for Jesus to find you.

This loop—this Guilt Loop—starts to break when you stop trying harder and start trusting deeper.

You're already forgiven. You're already free. Let that truth carry you.

Let grace do what guilt never could.

Chapter 7
THE COMPARISON CURSE
When someone else's life steals yours

Comparison doesn't always look like envy.
Sometimes it looks like the scroll—and feels like sinking.

You see someone else's joy and wonder where yours went.
Their story, their voice, their highlight reel—it all makes you question your own worth.
You scroll and smile, but deep down, something sinks.

You try to be grateful. You try to be content. But your soul feels like it's in someone else's shadow.

You stop showing up as yourself. And little by little, the life God gave you starts to feel like it's not enough.

That's the curse: someone else's blessing begins to feel like your burden.

How It Starts to Spiral

This loop begins with a glance—and grows in silence. Here's how it usually takes shape:

1. *You notice someone else's success.* A post. A conversation. A milestone.

2. *You internalize the gap.* Instead of celebrating, you compare—and come up short.

3. *You hide or hustle.* You either push harder to keep up, or pull away and stop trying.

4. *You lose your joy.* Nothing feels like enough. Even your wins feel small.

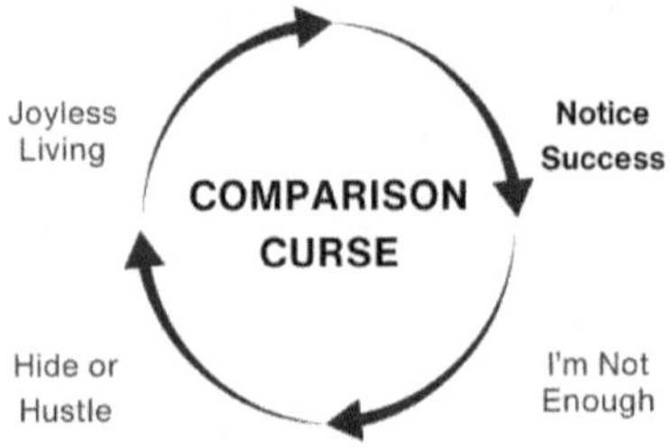

What starts with curiosity becomes criticism—usually toward yourself.

What's Still True About You

God never asked you to be them. He only ever asked you to be His.

You are fearfully and wonderfully made (Psalm 139:14).

You are uniquely placed in the body of Christ (1 Corinthians 12:18).

You are not a copy. You are not behind. You are not forgotten.
You don't need to outrun, outshine, or outperform.
You're not less than. You're not late.

You're already loved.

That's the truth that silences comparison. That's the truth that sets you free.

Someone Just Like You

After the resurrection, Jesus pulled Peter aside. He gave him forgiveness, restored his calling, and told him, *"Follow Me."*

But Peter looked at John and said, *"What about him?"* (John 21:21)

Even in the middle of his healing, Peter got distracted by someone else's story.

Jesus didn't scold him. He just said, *"What is that to you? You must follow Me."*

It wasn't harsh. It was holy.

Jesus wasn't comparing Peter and John. He was calling Peter back to his own path.
That's what He does with you, too.

And just like Peter, we often wander after clarity instead of Christ.

The Way Out Begins Here

You don't have to keep chasing a life that isn't yours.

You don't have to keep shrinking to fit someone else's story.

If you're ready to step out of the loop, start here:

- *Look at what's in your hands.* What's already growing? What's already good?
- *Name your lane.* Where has God placed you? What makes your heart come alive?
- *Celebrate on purpose.* Gratitude is the door that leads you home.

These aren't productivity hacks. They're posture shifts. Each one brings your heart back to center.

What fruit is already growing in your life that you've ignored because it wasn't someone else's?

Try These Prayers

When comparison whispers that you're behind or not enough, let truth speak louder. Let your breath bring you back to the ground God gave you.

A Breath Prayer

Inhale: I am uniquely made...

Exhale: ...I will walk my path.

A Prayer of Realignment

God,

I confess—I've looked too long at someone else's story.

I've measured myself by timelines and highlights You never asked me to chase.

I've forgotten the beauty You've placed in me.

Bring me back.

Help me see what You're doing in my life.

Teach me to celebrate others without losing sight of my own calling.

I want to follow You—eyes forward, heart open.

In Jesus' name, Amen.

Let this be your return to the path made just for you.

Where the Loop Starts to Break

You are not behind. You are not missing it. You are not invisible.

This loop—this Comparison Curse—starts to break the moment you stop asking, "What about them?" and start listening for, "Follow Me."

There's a garden in your lane.
There's peace in your pace.
There's purpose in your presence.

You don't have to chase what God never asked you to carry.
Just walk with Him. That's enough.

Chapter 8

THE FEAR LOOP

When fear pulls you away from love

Fear doesn't always look like panic. Sometimes it looks like silence. Or control. Or hesitation.

You feel the nudge to speak, to try, to go—but you freeze. You calculate the risk. You imagine everything that could go wrong. And before anything even happens, you've already pulled back.

You think you're protecting yourself. But you're actually building a cage.

Fear promises to keep you safe. But what it really keeps is your heart—locked up, worn out, and alone.

And it doesn't only keep you from pain—it keeps you from joy, too.

This loop doesn't just hold you back. It holds you hostage.

How It Starts to Spiral

Fear is rarely loud at first. It whispers, then it wraps around you. It grows in silence and shapes your decisions before you even realize it.

Here's how the spiral often begins:

1. *You sense a threat.* Something uncertain. Something hard. Your body tenses. Your breath shallows.

2. *You pull back.* You delay, avoid, or shrink. You sidestep conversations. You postpone action—just in case.

3. *You isolate.* You stay quiet. You feel the room close in. You start to believe that retreat is the only safe option.

4. *You lose your courage.* Doubt grows. Confidence shrinks. Fear starts to sound like wisdom—but it's only keeping you from what love could do.

By the time you realize it's a loop, you've already built your life around its limits.

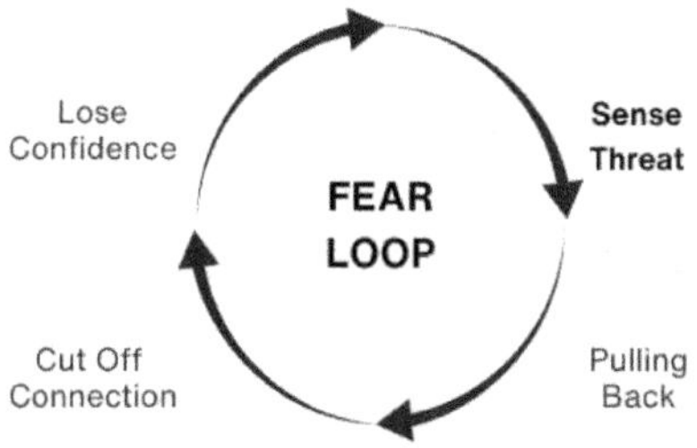

And now the world feels smaller. But God has more for you than safety.

What's Still True About You

You are not your fear. You are not fragile. And you are not walking alone.

The Bible says, *"God has not given us a spirit of fear, but of power, love, and a sound mind."* (2 Timothy 1:7)

You don't have to pretend to be fearless. You don't have to fake confidence.

You just have to take one small, surrendered step.

You are not defined by your hesitation—you are defined by His presence.

Even when you're trembling, God is steady. Even when your heart pounds, His hand holds.

The fear doesn't make you unworthy. The fear is just the place where faith gets to grow.

Someone Just Like You

There was a man in the tombs—naked, wild, and tormented. People avoided him. Fear had hollowed him out.

Then Jesus stepped on shore (Mark 5).

With one word, the torment lifted. The man was found sitting, clothed, and in his right mind.

But then something surprising happened: he begged to leave with Jesus.

And Jesus said no.

Instead, He gave him something better than escape—He gave him purpose.

"Go home to your own people and tell them how much the Lord has done for you."

Jesus didn't just calm the fear. He gave the man his life back. *And just like him, we often long for escape—when Jesus is offering restoration.*

That's what He offers you, too. Not just relief—but restoration.

The Way Out Begins Here

You don't have to wait until you're fearless to move forward. You can carry your fear—and still take the next step.

If you're ready to breathe again, to try again, to live again—start small.

- *Name the fear. Speak it out loud. Fear thrives in silence.*
- *Tell someone safe. Let someone witness what you've been holding alone.*
- *Do one small thing afraid. Think of it like opening a window—just enough to let light back in.*
- *Feel your feet on the floor. Let your breath come back slow.*

These steps won't make fear disappear. But they'll remind you that fear doesn't get to lead.

God does. And He's not in a hurry—but He is with you, waiting for your yes.

Try These Prayers

Fear talks fast. Jesus speaks slow. He's not trying to rush you—He's trying to walk with you. So breathe. Listen. Let your body remember who holds you.

A Breath Prayer

Inhale: I am not alone...

Exhale: ...I trust You here.

A Prayer of Courage

Lord, You know what I'm afraid of.

You see the stories I play in my head—the ones where everything breaks.

But I want to trust You more than I trust my fear.

I want to move even when I feel small.

So today, I bring You my shaking hands and my worried thoughts.

Lead me one step at a time.

Make me brave—not by removing fear,

but by filling me with Your presence.

In Jesus' name, Amen.

Let this prayer be your first small act of courage. You're not stepping out alone. You're stepping into the arms of the One who walks through valleys.

Where the Loop Starts to Break

You don't have to be fearless to move forward.

This loop—this Fear Loop—starts to break when you stop letting fear take the lead and *start following love instead.*

Courage doesn't mean the fear is gone.
It just means the fear doesn't get to drive.

He walks beside you—steady, shoulder to shoulder.

Step by step, the light grows.
And you'll remember how to walk through the dark—without flinching.

Chapter 9
THE SHAME LOOP
When you believe you are the problem

Shame is quieter than guilt—but it runs deeper.

Guilt says, *"I did something wrong."*

Shame says, *"I am wrong."*

You carry it like a secret. You've layered yourself in silence, hoping no one will see what's underneath.

It shows up when you try to be seen, when you try to belong, when you dare to believe you're lovable. It whispers that you're broken—not just a little, but at the core.

So you hide. You edit yourself. You silence your story.

You shrink in rooms where you used to laugh. You filter your words like you're walking on glass.

You pull back before anyone gets close enough to confirm what you already fear: *You are the problem.*

This isn't just about what happened to you. It's what you've come to believe about yourself.

And shame is relentless—until grace speaks louder. Louder than the lie. Louder than the silence.

How It Starts to Spiral

Shame doesn't always shout. Most of the time, it just settles in—quiet, but heavy.
It wraps around your identity and starts shaping how you show up—before you even realize it's there.

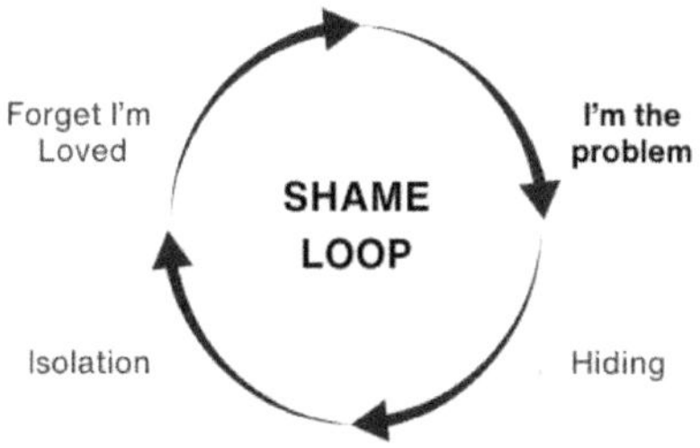

Here's how the spiral usually begins:

1. *You believe you're the problem.* Not just that you messed up—but that you *are* a mess. That your worth is tied to your worst moment, or someone else's words.

2. *You hide.* You edit yourself. You keep conversations shallow. You learn how to stay visible—but not truly seen.

3. *You isolate.* You avoid the places and people that might reflect back love. You convince yourself you're safer alone.

4. *You forget you're loved.* Not just by people—but by God. You start to believe that if He really saw everything, He might walk away too.

And by then, shame isn't just a feeling—it's a filter.
It colors how you hear encouragement. It dilutes your joy. It turns every kindness into suspicion.

But here's the truth:
God sees everything—and still chooses you.
He doesn't love a cleaned-up version of you. He loves the real you.
And that's where healing begins.

What's Still True About You

You are not the problem.

You are not what was done to you. You are not your worst decision. You are not the echo of what someone else said when they didn't see your worth.

You are God's beloved—created in His image and made new in His grace.

"Those who look to Him are radiant; their faces are never covered with shame." (Psalm 34:5)

Shame says, *"Hide."*

God says, *"Come."*

You don't have to clean yourself up. You just have to come as you are—and He will do the rest.

You're not too broken to be seen. You're not too far gone to be loved. And you're not beyond restoration.

This isn't about becoming someone new. It's about remembering who you've always been.

Someone Just Like You

She came in quietly, carrying a jar of perfume and a soul full of regret.

Everyone else saw her reputation. Jesus saw the ache in her eyes, the story in her tears.

She wept at His feet, wiped them with her hair, and poured out everything she had left (Luke 7).

The room judged her. Jesus welcomed her.

He didn't flinch. He didn't correct. He called it worship.

He said, *"Your sins are forgiven... Your faith has saved you. Go in peace."*

She didn't leave fixed. She left free.

Jesus wasn't afraid of her shame. And He's not afraid of yours.

He doesn't push away the ones who feel ruined. He invites them in closer.

The Way Out Begins Here

Shame says you have to hide. Grace says you can come into the light.

You don't have to fix yourself before you're welcome. You don't have to feel brave to begin.

If you're ready to loosen shame's grip, begin here:

- *Name what you believe about yourself.* Write it down. Say it out loud. Let it lose its power in the open.
- *Notice who you're avoiding.* Who are you afraid will see the real you?
- *Tell someone safe.* Not to fix it—but to remind you you're still worth loving.

These steps don't erase the past. But they open the door to healing.

Jesus never healed anyone who was pretending. He healed the ones who came close.

You can start with a whisper. He's already listening.

Try These Prayers

Shame grows in silence. But healing begins when you bring your whole self—unfiltered—to God. Let these prayers guide you back to the truth.

A Breath Prayer

Inhale: I am not what I've done...

Exhale: ...I am who You say I am.

A Prayer of Belonging

Jesus,

I've believed the lie that I am too broken to be loved.

I've hidden the parts of me I was sure would make You turn away.

But You keep reaching. You keep inviting.

So I'm coming—flaws and all.

Speak truth over my shame.

Remind me that I still belong.

I don't want to hide anymore.

In Your name, Amen.

Let this prayer peel back the layers—just enough for light to get in.

Where the Loop Starts to Break

You are not the problem.

You're not too much. You're not not enough.

This loop—this Shame Loop—starts to break when you stop hiding and start believing you're still worthy of being found.

Jesus already knows the real you. And He still chooses you.

Grace doesn't flinch. Love doesn't leave. And healing begins where you stop pretending.

You don't have to cover up anymore. You're already covered.

Your face can be radiant again—without shame.

Chapter 10

THE ANXIETY LOOP

When control wears out your soul

Anxiety doesn't always come as panic. Sometimes it shows up as planning. Or perfection. Or staying three steps ahead—just in case.

You feel the pressure to hold everything together, so you work harder. You overthink. You scan for what might go wrong and try to prevent it.

But instead of peace, you get more pressure.

This loop begins with anxiety but hides behind a composed face. You look steady, but inside, your thoughts are sprinting.

You're trying to stay in control. But what you're really doing is bracing yourself—every hour of every day.

And eventually, your soul starts to wear thin.

That's the Anxiety Loop. Not just fear of what's coming—but fear that who you are isn't enough to meet it.

How It Starts to Spiral

Anxiety loops don't start with failure—they start with fear. Here's how the pattern usually plays out:

1. *You feel uncertain.* A situation, a decision, or even just a silence stirs unease. You brace.

2. *You try to stay in control.* You plan more. Anticipate more. You take on what isn't yours to carry.

3. *You get soul fatigue.* Not just tired—but thin, like your spirit is fraying. Like you're made of thread, and every tug unravels something sacred. You rest, but never really exhale. The weariness doesn't sleep off—it settles in.

4. *You fear not measuring up.* You wonder if your best won't be good enough—so you push harder.

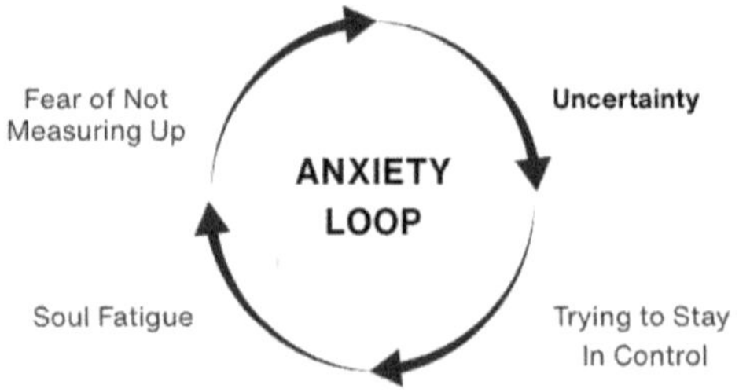

And the more exhausted you get, the more anxious you feel. The loop spins again—quicker, tighter, louder.

What's Still True About You

You don't have to manage everything to be okay.

"Cast all your anxiety on Him because He cares for you." (1 Peter 5:7)

God doesn't ask you to carry anxiety. He invites you to release it.

You are not your stress level. You are not your performance. You are not your ability to stay ahead.

- Even when your thoughts race, His presence remains.
- Even when you're anxious, you're held.
- Even when you're afraid, you're loved.
- Even when you can't slow your mind, you're safe.

He was there before the weight—and He'll still be there after it lifts.

You don't have to measure up. Jesus already did.

And even in your spiraling, you are not alone.

Someone Just Like You

Elijah had just experienced one of the most powerful miracles in Scripture—fire from heaven, a public victory for God. But the next day, he ran. Fear took over.

He collapsed under a tree and prayed, *"I have had enough, Lord."* (1 Kings 19:4)

He wasn't faithless. He was just... done. Spent. Empty.

He lay down in the wilderness under the weight of everything he couldn't fix. No more fire. No more calling. Just fear and fatigue.

And God let him sleep. Twice. Before He whispered truth, He whispered rest.

God didn't scold him. He didn't push him to do more.

Instead, God gave him food. Gave him space. Then met him again—not in wind, or fire, or earthquake—but in a whisper.

Elijah's anxiety wasn't proof he was weak. It was proof he was human.

And God met him with gentle strength.

The Way Out Begins Here

You don't have to earn rest. You don't have to fix everything before you exhale.

If anxiety has been your engine, here's where you can begin to slow the loop:

- *Name what's keeping you up at night.* Get specific. Don't filter it—just say it out loud or write it down.
- *Lay down the outcome.* Ask God, *"What am I trying to control that You've already claimed?"*
- *Choose one thing to leave undone.* Not everything. Just one thing. Let it stay unfinished as an act of trust.
- *Let someone in.* Not to solve it—but to witness it. You weren't meant to carry this alone.

These aren't steps to fix you. They're steps to return you to peace.

The Bible says,

> *"Do not be anxious about anything, but in every situation, by prayer and petition, with thanksgiving, present your requests to God." And the peace of God, which transcends all understanding, will guard your hearts and your minds in Christ Jesus. (Philippians 4:6–7)*

Let that peace meet you here.

Try These Prayers

Anxiety runs fast. Let's slow it down.

Let your body catch up with what your spirit already knows: You are not alone.

You don't need the perfect words—just a real heart. Let these prayers give you space to breathe again.

A Breath Prayer

Inhale: You hold what I can't...

Exhale: ...I give You what I've gripped too long.

Another Breath Prayer

Inhale: You're already here...

Exhale: ...I choose to trust.

A Prayer of Trust

Jesus,

You know how I spiral.

I carry things I can't control.

I try to fix what was never mine to fix.

But I want something better than this loop.

I want to trust You.

So right now, I give You what's too heavy.

Teach me how to rest inside Your care.

Even if my mind races, let my soul be held. Let my breath remind my body I'm safe. You are before me. You are behind me. You are with me now.

In Your name, Amen.

Let this be your breath-break. You don't have to hold what God is already handling.

Where the Loop Starts to Break

You don't have to be fearless to feel peace.

You just need to loosen your grip.

This loop—this Anxiety Loop—starts to break when you stop trying to hold it all and start trusting the One who already does.

Peace isn't the absence of pressure. It's the presence of God in the middle of it.

You're not behind. You're not broken. You're just tired.
And the One who said, *"Come to Me, all who are weary,"* still means it.

Unclench. Breathe. Let go. God is already holding the rest.

Chapter 11

THE JUDGMENT LOOP

When insecurity turns into criticism

Judgment doesn't always sound angry. Sometimes it sounds spiritual. Or clever. Or like just being honest.

But underneath the sharp words and quick opinions is something far more tender: fear. Fear that you're not enough. That you're being evaluated. That if you're not right, you're not worth it.

So you compare. You critique. You tighten the lens. You label what you don't understand.

Somewhere along the way, you learned to judge—so you wouldn't feel judged.

Judgment is like a cracked mirror. It reflects just enough to recognize yourself, but distorts everything you see.

Sometimes you turn it on others. Sometimes you turn it on yourself. Either way, it creates distance from the people you were meant to love—and from the grace you were meant to receive.

Judgment builds walls. Grace opens windows.

It feels like power. But it's actually a prison.

You don't feel free. You feel tight.

This is the judgment loop. And it doesn't break with better arguments. It breaks with mercy.

How It Starts to Spiral

This loop often feels justified—until you realize it's keeping you stuck. Here's how it quietly builds:

1. *You feel insecure.* You wonder if you're doing enough, being enough, seen enough.

2. *You compare.* Sideways glances become measurements. You start ranking where you fall.

3. *You criticize others—or yourself.* You name the flaw before it names you. It feels like control, but it's actually protection.

4. *You lose sight of grace.* You forget what it feels like to be forgiven, to be chosen, to be safe. And that forgetfulness hardens your voice.

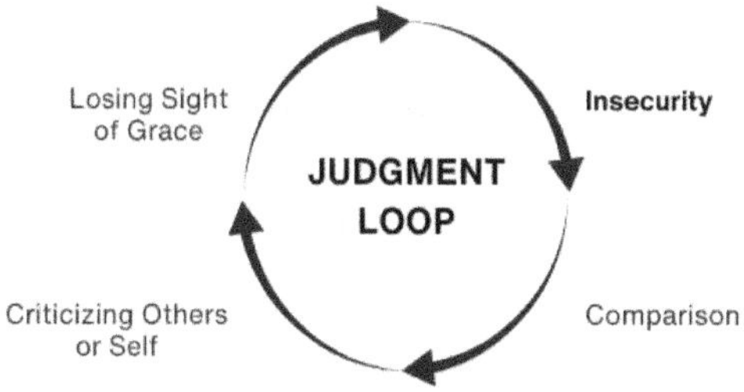

The longer you stay in the loop, the more critical you become—and the less connected you feel.

What's Still True About You

You don't have to protect yourself with critique.

You're already covered by grace.

The judgment that could have fallen on you—already fell on Jesus. What's left now is mercy.

Mercy triumphs over judgment. (James 2:13)

You don't need to win the comparison game to be secure in God's love.

You don't need to spot the flaw to stay safe. You don't need to correct the room to be seen.

He already chose you. Already loves you. Already welcomes you into His kindness.

You're not disqualified because you've been defensive.

You're not too sharp to soften. You're not too hardened to heal.

Judgment builds walls. Mercy builds bridges.

And you were made to walk in grace—not just to receive it, but to give it.

Someone Just Like You

A Pharisee stood tall in the temple, confident and composed.

"God, I thank You that I'm not like other people..." (Luke 18:11)

Across the room, a tax collector stood far off. His head stayed low. His eyes stayed down. He beat his chest and whispered,

"God, have mercy on me, a sinner."

Imagine that room—the space between them. The silence. The tension. One man needed no help. The other hoped for it with all his heart.

Only one of them left right with God—and it wasn't the one with all the answers.

Jesus said,

"Those who exalt themselves will be humbled, and those who humble themselves will be exalted."

Judgment hardens. Humility heals.

And mercy is still waiting for those who know they need it.

The Way Out Begins Here

You don't have to protect yourself by tearing others down. You don't have to stay sharp to feel safe.

Judgment loses its grip when mercy is chosen on purpose.

If you're ready to soften, try this:

- *Catch the voice.* Notice that quick critique—whether toward others or yourself.
- *Replace it with kindness.* Ask, *"What would grace say here?"* Then say that instead.
- *Practice blessing.* Speak life over someone you'd rather avoid. Not to impress God—but to join Him.
- *Sit in silence.* Before responding. Before correcting. Let mercy have a moment to speak before you do.

These aren't performance tasks. They're postures of freedom.

And you don't need to do them all at once. Just start with the one that feels hardest.

Try These Prayers

Judgment protects—but it also isolates. It walls off your tenderness and whispers that it's strength. But grace is stronger.

Let this be a moment to soften your inner voice and let mercy back in.

A Breath Prayer

Inhale: I choose mercy...

Exhale: ...I lay down judgment.

A Prayer of Softening

Jesus,

I've learned to spot what's wrong—sometimes before I even notice what's good.

I've used judgment to feel in control.

But it's making me hard inside.

I don't want to live like this.

Teach me how to trade criticism for compassion.

Help me speak to others—and to myself—with kindness.

Let mercy lead me home.

In Your name, Amen.

Let this prayer be your turning point—like opening a window after too long indoors. A place where grace gets the final say.

Where the Loop Starts to Break

You don't have to be right to be loved.

You don't have to critique to feel safe.

This loop—this Judgment Loop—starts to break when you stop leading with opinion and start listening with grace.

Judgment is a cracked mirror. Grace is a window.

Mercy still opens the door.

And your reflection gets clearer as you walk through.

The world doesn′t need sharper voices. It needs softer hearts.

Start there. Start with yours.

Chapter 12
THE TRAUMA LOOP
When the past hijacks the present

Trauma doesn't just remember—it relives.

It plays like a film you didn't ask to see, triggered by something you didn't even notice. Suddenly, your heart races. Your breath shortens. Your body tenses, even when nothing's wrong right now.

You're not weak. You're wired to survive—but what helped you survive is not meant to lead you forever.

But over time, what helped you survive starts to control you.

You avoid. You numb. You shut down.

You build a life that feels safer—but also smaller.

You laugh, but not too loud. You love, but not too close.

It's not that you don't care—it's that caring feels like a risk your nervous system can't afford.

You start reacting to life from behind a thick glass wall—seeing everything, but feeling nothing.

That's the Trauma Loop. The moment is over—but your body doesn't know that yet.

And until it does, the past keeps interrupting the present.

How It Starts to Spiral

Trauma loops begin with something real—*Old Pain.* It may be a moment, a season, or a wound that was never given space to heal.

Then comes the *Overwhelmed Reaction.* You feel unsafe or out of control. Your body reacts like the danger is happening all over again—even if you're just standing in line or having a normal conversation.

Shame creeps in next. Not just about what happened—but how your body responded, and how long it's taken to "get over it."

Then you enter *Avoidance.* People. Places. Emotions. You keep your world small, thinking it'll keep you safe.

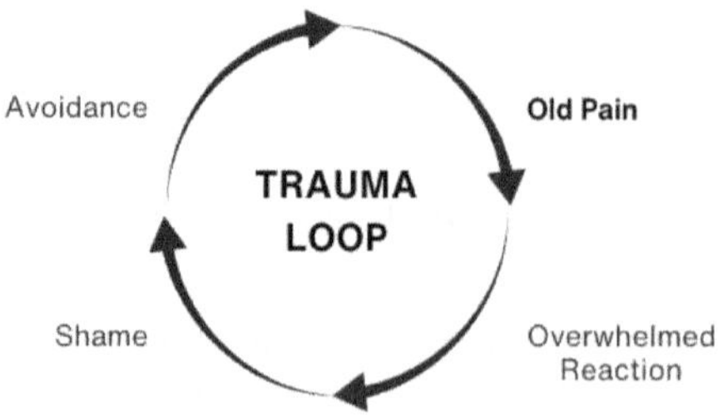

But the pain doesn't stay away. It stays buried—and anything buried alive still finds ways to surface.

What's Still True About You

You are not your trauma.

You are not what happened to you. You are not what you had to do to survive.

God doesn't rush your healing. He's not frustrated by your fear. He's patient. Gentle. Near.

"The Lord is close to the brokenhearted and saves those who are crushed in spirit." (Psalm 34:18)

God is not pacing. He's not impatient.

He's sitting with you like someone who knows what silence sounds like on the other side of pain.

Your reactions don't disqualify you.

Your triggers don't define you.

Your pain is not a problem to fix—it's a wound to bring into the light.

You don't have to be fully healed to be fully loved.

Panic isolates. Presence restores. Grace waits.

And you don't have to carry the past alone anymore.

Someone Just Like You

The man with the legion of demons lived in the tombs—naked, isolated, tormented (Mark 5). People avoided him. He avoided himself.

His pain was more than physical. He was chained from the inside out.

But when Jesus stepped onto the shore, the man ran toward Him. Not away.

Even in his torment, something in him knew Jesus was safe.

Jesus didn't flinch. He didn't correct. He called the man out of the chaos and into his right mind.

The townspeople saw the difference.

The man sat—clothed, calm, and whole.

Jesus didn't just heal him. He gave him back his dignity.

The Way Out Begins Here

You don't have to relive it to release it.

But you do have to stop pretending it didn't shape you.

Healing begins with honesty—not performance.

If the past is still echoing, try this:

- *Notice what stirs your panic.* Write it down. Trace it gently. Ask, "What does this remind me of?"
- *Ground yourself in the present.* Look around. Name five things you can see. Feel your feet on the floor. Breathe slow.
- *Speak to your younger self.* The one who was scared. The one who went quiet. Say, "You're safe now. We made it through."
- *Invite Jesus into the memory.* Not to erase it, but to stay until the pain no longer drives the story.

You don't have to feel brave to take the first step.

You just have to stop walking alone.

Try These Prayers

Your story doesn't disqualify you. It's where Jesus meets you.

Let these prayers begin to unfreeze what's been buried too long.

A Breath Prayer

Inhale: I am not what happened to me...

Exhale: ...I am safe in You.

Let your breath become the doorway back to safety.

A Prayer of Safety

Jesus,

You know what I've carried.

You know where I was hurt, where I went silent, where I learned to hide.

I don't want to keep living from that place.

I want to heal.

Be near me when the past rises again.

Be gentle with the parts of me still afraid.

Show me how to live from peace, not panic.

In Your name, Amen.

You don't have to rush healing.

But you can start talking to the One who never left.

Where the Loop Starts to Break

You are not stuck in survival mode forever.

This loop—this Trauma Loop—starts to break when you stop blaming yourself for how you learned to cope.

The moment is over. But healing is still unfolding.

And Jesus is still present in both.

You don't have to be fully healed to be fully loved.

You don't have to keep living behind the glass wall. Jesus breaks the glass gently—from the inside out. The moment doesn't disappear. But your isolation starts to.

Stay here. Stay honest. Stay close.

Jesus already is.

Chapter 13

THE IDENTITY LOOP

When shame rewrites your name

This loop doesn't come from a single moment—it comes from the story you started telling yourself when the shame sank in.

You don't just feel like you messed up—you start to believe you are a mess.

It sounds like, "This is just who I am."

It feels like something renamed you—quietly, painfully, without permission.

So you shrink. Or you perform. Or you hide behind a version of you that gets approval—even if it's not the real you.

This isn't insecurity. It's identity confusion.

You forgot who you are.

Or maybe, you never really knew.

Judgment builds walls. Grace opens the door.

How It Starts to Spiral

It starts with a *Mistake*. A failure, a fall, or something someone said that left a mark.

You turn inward with *Self-Shaming*. Not just, *"I messed up,"* but *"I'm a mess."* You rehearse the labels, believing them more each time.

Then you *Pull Away*. You stop showing up fully. You keep the real parts of you hidden. You assume people wouldn't love the you behind the mask.

You still show up, but not fully. You talk, but only in safe tones.

You tell parts of your story—never the whole thing.

You live near people, but not with them. And eventually, the version you're pretending to be becomes the only one anyone knows.

Eventually, you *Stop Believing You Can Grow*. You think this is just who you are now. That healing is for other people. That maybe change isn't possible for someone like you.

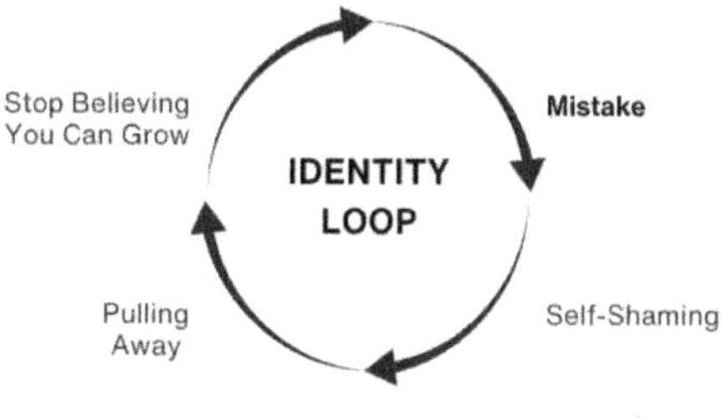

But none of that is true. It just feels true when shame gets to write your story.

What's Still True About You

You are not the worst thing you've done.
You are not the lie you've believed the longest.

You are not broken beyond repair. You are not a lost cause. You are not unlovable.

You are God's workmanship—His design, His delight, His image-bearer.

See what great love the Father has lavished on us,
that we should be called children of God!
And that is what we are!" (1 John 3:1)

You are not a sticker someone slapped on you.
You are a hand-lettered signature—written by grace, sealed with love.

The voice of shame tells you who you're not.
The voice of God reminds you who you've always been.

You're still becoming. Still unfolding. Still beloved.
And your name is still safe in His hands.

Someone Just Like You

The woman at the well came alone. In the heat of the day. When no one else would be there.
The sun pressed down. The stones burned underfoot.
She wasn't just thirsty—she was tired of being a name people whispered.

But Jesus met her there. Not with shame. Not with accusation. With presence.

He named her truth—but not to expose her. To free her.
She'd been told her whole life what she wasn't.
But Jesus told her who she was.

"You have had five husbands... and the man you now have is not your husband."

Still, He stayed.
Still, He spoke.

And she ran back to town—not with her head down, but with her heart open.
The woman who once hid became the first to tell her whole village who Jesus really was.

The Way Out Begins Here

You can stop rehearsing who you're not.
You can start reclaiming who you are.

This isn't about pretending you're perfect. It's about remembering you're known.

If shame has renamed you, try this:

- *Name the lie.* Write down the false label you've carried. Say it out loud. Let it lose its grip.
- *Return to the truth.* What does God call you? (Loved. Chosen. Daughter. Son. Seen.)

- *Let someone see the real you.* No mask. No polish. Just honest presence with someone safe.
- *Do one small thing as your true self.* Not to prove anything—but to remember you don't have to disappear.

You're not building something new. You're remembering what's been true all along.

Try These Prayers

You're not too far gone to come home to who you are.

Let these prayers remind you of the name that never changed.

A Breath Prayer

Inhale: I am who You say I am...

Exhale: ...I let go of every false name.

Let your breath be the sound of coming home.

A Prayer of Restoration

Let this prayer be the sound of coming home to who you are—the quiet place where grace gets the final word.

Father,

I've called myself things You never would.

I've worn labels that never fit.

I've tried to be someone I'm not, just to feel worthy.

But You know me. And You still choose me.

Speak over my identity until the truth feels real again.

Help me live like I'm already loved.

Let my name echo Yours.

In Jesus' name, Amen.

Let this prayer be the sound of your real name, spoken in the silence where shame once shouted.

Where the Loop Starts to Break

You don't have to keep pretending.

This loop—this *Identity Loop*—starts to break the moment you stop trying to become someone else and start remembering who you've always been.

You don't need to fix your name. You just need to come home to it.
You don't need a new title. Just a fresh reminder of the one that never changed.

And the Father who named you?
He's already running toward you.

Chapter 14
THE CONTROL LOOP
When doing more never feels like enough

Control often disguises itself as responsibility. It doesn't always look like dominance—it can feel like clenched fists, a jaw that won't relax, a brain that won't stop buzzing.

You're not trying to dominate—you're just trying to hold it all together. For everyone. All the time.

You plan. You overwork. You stay five steps ahead. You handle things so no one else has to.

But underneath the organization and the effort is a quiet panic:

If I let go, it might all fall apart.

Or worse—*I* might fall apart.

You're spinning so many plates, terrified that if one drops, it's not just the task that shatters—it's your worth.

So you do more. Push harder. Hide how tired you are.

You measure your worth by your output. You tie peace to your performance. But deep down, you know—it's not sustainable.

No matter how much you do, it never feels like enough.

That's not strength.

That's the control loop—where peace is always just one task away.

How It Starts to Spiral

Control often starts in a good place. You want to serve. To help. To carry your part.

But when pressure becomes your default, and perfection becomes the goal, the spiral begins.

Here's how this loop usually unfolds:

1. *You feel perfection pressure.* Not from everyone else—but from yourself. You believe things must be flawless to be okay.

2. *You start overworking.* Tasks multiply. Stillness feels unsafe. Rest feels like failure.

3. *You feel like you're never enough.* Even when you do well, it still doesn't feel like it's enough to earn rest or love.

4. *You blame yourself.* For not doing more. For not doing it better. You carry guilt for simply being tired.

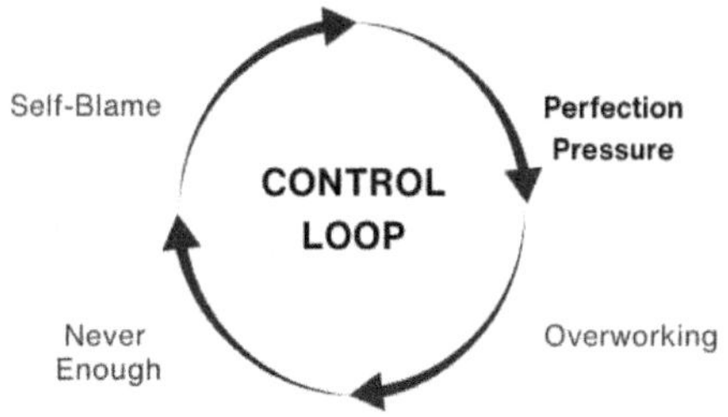

And instead of stepping back, you step harder on the gas. That's how control reinforces itself—until you no longer remember what freedom feels like.

What's Still True About You

You were never meant to carry it all.

God didn't design you to be the solution to every problem or the strength behind every system. He made you to be held.

> *"Come to Me, all who are weary and burdened,*
> *and I will give you rest." (Matthew 11:28)*

Control says, *"If I don't hold it together, everything will fall apart."*

But grace says, *"Let go. I'm already holding you."*

You are not cherished for your output. You are not safe because you perform. You're safe because you're His.

And God never asked you to be invincible. He asked you to be present—with Him, with others, with yourself.

You can trade the weight for rest. You can lay down the pressure and still be loved.

Someone Just Like You

Naaman was a commander—respected, decorated, and in control. But underneath the armor, he had leprosy. And when he finally went to Elisha for healing, he expected something dramatic.

Instead, the prophet told him to do something small: *"Go wash in the Jordan seven times."* (2 Kings 5)

Naaman was furious. It didn't feel big enough. Didn't feel powerful. He almost walked away.

But one of his servants said, *"If the prophet had told you to do something great, wouldn't you have done it?"*

So Naaman let go of the plan. He dipped in the river. And he came up clean.

What changed him wasn't the water. It was the release.

God didn't ask Naaman to solve the problem. He just asked him to surrender.

Like Naaman, your surrender might feel too small to matter—but it's where healing begins.

The Way Out Begins Here

It's okay to loosen your grip. You don't have to be the strong one.

You weren't made to carry what hasn't happened yet. You can begin to let go—slowly, kindly, honestly.

Let this be the holy unraveling—where you stop managing and start trusting. If you're ready, try this:

- *Notice where you're over-functioning.* Where are you always the first to speak, the last to leave, the one still fixing while everyone else rests?
- *Loosen one grip.* Delegate. Rest. Delete the extra. Let one thing stay undone.
- *Let God interrupt you.* Stop mid-scroll. Pause mid-task. Say, *"God, what do You want to hold for me today?"*
- *Name one fear.* Say it out loud. Not to give it power—but to give it a place to leave.

These aren't steps to fix yourself. They're invitations to breathe again.

You've held so much for so long. Let today be the first thread you release—the beginning of untangling what was never yours to hold.

Try These Prayers

Control feels safe—but grace is lighter. You weren't made to hold it all. Let this be a breath-sized moment to release what you never had to carry.

A Breath Prayer

Inhale: I don't have to do it all...

Exhale: ...You're already holding me.

A Prayer of Surrender

God,

I'm afraid of what might happen if I stop. You know how much I've tried to manage.

I've planned, I've pushed, I've performed. But I'm tired.

I don't want to run on pressure anymore. Help me release what's not mine to hold.

Remind me I'm loved—whether or not I finish the list.

Teach me to trust You more than I trust my plans.

In Jesus' name, Amen.

Let this be your pause—a holy interruption where peace begins.

Where the Loop Starts to Break

You're not holding the world together. That was never your job.

This loop—this Control Loop—starts to break the moment you loosen your grip and open your hands.

God isn't waiting for your perfection. He's waiting for your surrender.

You don't need a blueprint for every hour, every problem, every tomorrow.

Let go of the weight. Let go of the pace. Let God hold what you've white-knuckled in fear.

Freedom doesn't always feel strong. Sometimes, it feels like rest.

Chapter 15
THE GRIEF LOOP
When numbness delays the mourning

Grief isn't just sadness.
It's the ache that follows any kind of loss—big or small, sudden or slow. A lost person. A lost place. A lost sense of how things were supposed to be.

Sometimes grief shows up as sobbing.
Sometimes it hides behind silence.
It doesn't always shout. Sometimes it just *sits there*—a quiet weight in your chest, a fog in your brain, a stillness that won't break.

You move through the motions.
You answer texts. You fold laundry. You show up for people.
But somewhere inside, something's frozen.

You're not broken.
You're just grieving.
That's the Grief Freeze.

It doesn't always look like pain. Sometimes, it just feels like pause.
You didn't ask to carry it. But here it is—quiet, heavy, waiting.
And no matter how long it's been, your soul still remembers.

How It Starts to Spiral

It begins with *Loss*. Someone or something you loved is gone. A person. A place. A season. A hope you carried close.

Then comes *Shock*.
Not always dramatic—sometimes it's subtle.
A mental fog. A numb stare. Days that pass without you really noticing. You smile, but it doesn't reach your eyes. You function, but you're not fully there.

Then comes *Emotional Numbing*.
Not because you don't care, but because your system doesn't know what to do with all the ache. You stop crying—not out of strength, but out of shutdown. You feel flat. Maybe even functional. But not fully alive.

And slowly, you begin to *Disconnect*.
From others. From yourself. From God.
You scroll instead of speak. You stay busy instead of still. You don't let yourself cry—because you're not sure what would happen if you started.

You start skipping conversations.
You nod through check-ins.

You smile when asked how you're doing—but not because you're okay. You just don't want to explain the ache.

Your world feels foggy, and you wonder if anyone notices you drifting.
The loop doesn't scream.
It *silences.*

What's Still True About You

You are not wrong for feeling this slowly.
You're not faithless because you're grieving.

Even if it's been years—
Even if the world moved on—
Your pain still matters to God.

Jesus didn't rush past sorrow.
He stepped into it.
He didn't scold Mary when she wept. He didn't rush Martha when she accused. He didn't give sermons. He gave space.

"Blessed are those who mourn, for they will be comforted." (Matthew 5:4)

Your grief isn't weakness.
It's love that has nowhere else to go yet.
Your numbness doesn't mean you're heartless.
It means your heart is trying to protect something fragile.

And even in the stillness—even in the sorrow—*you are still held.*

God isn't asking you to snap out of it.

He's asking you to *let Him sit with you in it.*

Someone Just Like You

Mary Magdalene stood outside the tomb, weeping.

Her hope had been buried.

Her healer, gone.

Her heart, broken.

She looked inside the grave—but couldn't see through the tears.

Even when Jesus stood near, she didn't recognize Him.

Grief has a way of clouding the familiar.

But then—

He said her name.

"Mary." (John 20:16)

And everything shifted.

Not because the pain was gone.

But because *presence* changed the room.

Jesus didn't wait for her to stop crying.

He met her right there—in the middle of her mourning.

He didn't rush her through it.

He *spoke her name back into the light.*

And that's what grief still needs—*not fixing, but naming. Not answers, but nearness.*

The Way Out Begins Here

You don't have to feel it all at once.
And you don't have to stay frozen forever.

Grief isn't a problem to fix.
It's a weight to *honor.*

If your sorrow has gone silent, try this:

- *Name the loss.* Say what you lost—out loud, on paper, or in prayer. Let it be specific.
- *Mark it with intention.* Light a candle. Revisit a place. Lay a stone. Write a letter. Create a small ritual that acknowledges, *"This mattered."*
- *Feel one part of it.* A photo. A memory. A moment. Give yourself permission to feel whatever surfaces—without needing to fix it.
- *Let God sit with you there.* No correcting. No pushing. Just presence. Let Him witness the ache.

You don't need permission to mourn.
But just in case—*this is it.* You're allowed.

Try These Prayers

You don't have to hold it together.

These prayers aren't for performance. They're for presence.

They don't require answers. Just honesty. Just breath. Just room.

A Breath Prayer

Inhale: I am allowed to grieve...

Exhale: ...You are here in the ache.

Let your breath remind you—*you don't cry alone.*

Every sigh is sacred. Every tear, noticed.

You're not invisible. You're not too much. You're not too late.

A Prayer of Honest Grief

God,

I don't always know what to feel.

Sometimes I'm numb. Sometimes I'm undone.

But You're still here.

You don't rush me. You don't push me past the pain.

Help me feel what I need to feel.

And when I can't feel anything at all—just stay with me.

Hold me in the hollow places.

Whisper hope where I can't find any.

In Jesus' name, Amen.

Let this prayer melt the silence—just enough for love to speak again.

Where the Loop Starts to Break

You're not too late to feel it.

You're not too broken to heal it.

And you were never meant to carry grief alone.

This loop—this Grief Freeze—starts to break when you let your heart thaw, one honest moment at a time.

Tears are not a sign of failure.

They're a language God understands.

The tears don't erase the loss.

But they begin to melt what's been frozen far too long.

And the God who weeps with you?

He's still near.

Even now.

Even here.

Chapter 16
THE LIES THAT LOOP US
Twelve traps we fall into—and the truth that sets us free

What if the loop isn't who you are... just what you believed?

We don't spiral because we're weak. We spiral because we're trying.
Trying to cope. Trying to stay safe. Trying to make it all make sense.

But the harder we try, the deeper we sink into emotional loops that lie to us.

Each one whispers a half-truth that sounds holy. Each one promises control, connection, or peace. But none of them deliver.

They don't just become habits. They become false gospels.

Jesus doesn't just correct the lie. He enters the loop. He names the ache. And He speaks a better word—not just to inform, but to transform.

What follows is a gentle walk through twelve loops many of us know by heart.
Each begins with a subtle lie that seems like self-protection—but ends up stealing our peace.

These are the old songs that kept us safe. But they're off-key. They wear us down.

Side-by-side with each loop, you'll see what Jesus says instead. Not as rebuke—but as rescue.
Not to shame the spiral—but to soften it.

Let truth rewrite what the lie tried to steal.

1. Anger Armor: How Blame Masks the Pain Beneath

- *False Gospel:* "My anger is justified—and necessary."
- *True Gospel:* "God's justice doesn't need my fury."

Anger may feel like strength. But it often guards a wound that never got time to weep.

Jesus doesn't shame our emotion. He invites us to grieve what hurt us—so we don't keep hurting others.

2. The People-Pleasing Loop: Burning Out to Be Loved

- *False Gospel:* "If I make everyone happy, I'll be safe."
- *True Gospel:* "Jesus didn't come to make everyone happy—He came to set hearts free."

Approval isn't peace. It's a treadmill.
Jesus doesn't require you to be agreeable. He invites you to be honest—with love.

3. The Guilt Loop: When Self-Punishment Feels Holy

- *False Gospel:* "If I suffer enough, God will forgive me."
- *True Gospel:* "Jesus already paid the full price."

Shame-driven guilt keeps us in motion. Grace invites us to rest.

You don't have to keep bleeding to prove you're sorry. The cross was enough.

4. The Comparison Curse: Measuring Yourself Into Misery

- *False Gospel:* "At least I'm doing better than they are."
- *True Gospel:* "God's grace isn't a contest—it's a gift."

Comparison tries to be a compass. But it only leads to loneliness.

Jesus levels the ground—not to flatten us, but to free us.

5. The Fear Loop: When Withdrawal Feels Safer Than Risk

- *False Gospel:* "If I try, I'll fail. If I speak, I'll be misunderstood. If I care, I'll get hurt."
- *True Gospel:* "Jesus doesn't wait at the top—He walks with me in the valley."

Fear sounds like wisdom. But it keeps us from living.

Jesus doesn't force us forward. He walks beside us until we're ready to move.

[Pause Here: Selah]

Let your heart breathe.

Midway through this list, it may feel heavy. Let grace settle in. None of this is about fixing yourself. It's about seeing clearly.

Now breathe again—and let truth speak.

6. The Shame Loop: When Failure Becomes Identity

- *False Gospel:* "I'm nothing. I'll never be enough for God."
- *True Gospel:* "Jesus became nothing so I could be made whole."

Shame says, "Hide."
Jesus says, "Come."

He doesn't erase your past to love you. He loves you into a new one.

7. The Anxiety Loop: When Control Becomes a Cage

- *False Gospel:* "If I worry enough, I'll be ready."
- *True Gospel:* "Jesus holds what I can't control."

Anxiety always has another task, another what-if, another reason to tense.

But peace doesn't come from fixing everything. It comes from letting Jesus carry what we never could.

8. The Judgment Loop: When Comparison Replaces Compassion

- *False Gospel:* "At least I'm doing better than they are."
- *True Gospel:* "God's grace isn't a contest—it's a gift."

Judgment hardens our words and narrows our world.

Grace invites us to open the window—to see others as God sees us: needing mercy, and worthy of it.

9. The Trauma Loop: When the Past Hijacks the Present

- *False Gospel:* "What happened to me defines who I am."
- *True Gospel:* "Jesus redeems my past and restores my identity."

The wound may still sting. But it no longer names you.

Jesus enters the memory—not to erase it, but to reclaim it.

10. The Identity Loop: When Shame Rewrites Your Name

- *False Gospel:* "I have to earn my place with God."
- *True Gospel:* "Jesus names me before I do anything."

Identity isn't something you build.
It's something you remember.

God never stopped calling you His.

11. The Control Loop: When Perfection Blocks Peace

- *False Gospel:* "If I get it right, I'll finally feel at peace."
- *True Gospel:* "God gives peace when I surrender, not when I perform."

Perfection is a performance. Surrender is a song.

Let grace lead the melody. Let rest be the refrain.

12. The Grief Loop: When Numbness Delays the Mourning

- *False Gospel:* "I shouldn't still feel this."
- *True Gospel:* "Jesus weeps with me, not against me."

Grief isn't a detour.
It's sacred ground.

Jesus doesn't rush your sorrow. He joins you in it—and gently leads you through.

Where the Loops Begin to Break

Every loop tries to name you.
Every lie tries to label you.

But Jesus speaks a better word.

He doesn't just cancel the spiral. He enters it.
Not to shame. To shepherd.

You don't have to prove your way out.
You just have to turn.

Because grace isn't behind you—it's coming toward you.

Loop by loop.
Lie by lie.
Step by step.

Jesus walks with you—not just out of what was,
but into the truest version of who you've always been.

❖

You don′t have to feel ready. You already are. —Jesus

Part 4

When Healing Becomes a Way of Life

If the last section helped you name your loops—if it gave shape to the silent struggles you've carried—this next part is about *how* you live now.
Not perfectly. Not all at once.
But forward. Gently. With Jesus.

You don't have to rush. But you're not stuck either.
You've walked some sacred ground already.
You slowed down.
You told the truth.
You let Jesus in.

And now something new begins—not because you've finally arrived, but because your soul has started to remember its shape.
The shape of peace.
The shape of grace.
The shape of being held.

Healing isn't just something that happens *in* you—it's something that takes root *through* you.
It becomes how you breathe. How you bless.
How you show up safe—for others, and for yourself.

This part of the journey isn't a checklist.
It's a rhythm.
A way of walking that stays soft and surrendered—even in a loud world.
A way of living open—even with a history of hiding.
A way of loving deep—even when it feels risky.

You don't have to get it right.
You just have to keep moving toward the warmth of grace.

So let's walk forward—slowly, kindly, together.
Heart still tender.
Hands open wide.
Jesus already with us.

Chapter 17
Keep the Soil Soft

I will give you a new heart and put a new spirit in you; I will remove from you your heart of stone and give you a heart of flesh.

—Ezekiel 36:26—

Some hearts don't close from rebellion. They close from exhaustion.

There's a kind of pain that doesn't explode—it sinks. Quietly. Slowly. It settles deep and hardens like dry ground left untended. Not angry. Just done.

A man once told me, "I don't feel angry anymore. But I don't feel much of anything." He'd prayed before. Trusted before. But nothing seemed to grow. So the soil of his soul dried out—brittle, untouched.

But the Gardener didn't leave.

God works with broken ground. He kneels in the dust and starts again. Not with force—but with kindness. With water. With time.

When the Ground Feels Dry

Picture a field after a long summer. Cracks forming. The last rain long forgotten. Beneath it all, something waits—a root, a promise.

The ground doesn't need force. It needs water. Time. And the hope that rain will return.

Healing doesn't come all at once. It starts with staying open—even when you feel nothing, even when the past whispers, "Why bother?"

God doesn't rush hard ground. He waters it.

And if you listen closely in the dry seasons, you might still hear Him. *Not in thunder—but in breath. Not in pressure—but in peace.*

Hearing the Voice That Still Speaks

When the soil is stiff, it can be hard to tell what's God... and what's just noise. Doubt. Fear. Static from old pain. But even in the drought, He still speaks. His voice still waters what feels withered.

If you're unsure how to listen again, try this:

- *Seek silence. Turn off the noise, even just for a moment.*
- *Test what you hear. God never contradicts His Word.*
- *Ask the Spirit to sort the noise from the truth.*
- *Talk to someone wise—someone who knows Scripture and knows your heart.*

These small practices begin to till the soil again. Little by little, the whisper sounds clearer.

When You Start to Feel Numb

Here's what to watch for—not as judgment, but as gentle alerts:

- You start dismissing spiritual things.
- Your words feel sharper than your heart intended.
- Worship feels like a memory—like watching someone else sing through a window.
- And prayer? Like knocking on a door that won't open.

These aren't signs of rebellion. They're signs your soul may be stiffening. That's when it's time to soften—not by striving, but by yielding.

Picture your fists unclenching. Your jaw loosening. Your shoulders releasing.

You may think, "I already worked through this."

But healing isn't linear. Most healing doesn't happen in one deep dig. It comes through slow, faithful tilling.

This isn't about trying harder. It's about loosening your grip and letting grace hold you.

A Gentle Way to Begin Again

You don't need to feel everything all at once.

You don't need to force the soil of your soul to change overnight.

You just need to stay open—honest enough, still enough—for the Gardener to begin again.

Here's a simple rhythm to try this week:

- *Morning Check-In:* Rest your hand over your heart. Ask, "Where am I closing up today?"
- *Evening Honesty:* Write one true sentence—no more. Let it stay raw. Let it lead you into stillness. *Example: "Today I feel dull."*

Or try this:

- Set a timer for two minutes.
- Sit in silence.
- Listen to your breath or your heartbeat. Let it remind you: *Life still moves beneath the surface. Even a seed cracks before it grows.*

Carry this breath prayer into your day:

> *Inhale:* Jesus, make me open...
> *Exhale:* ...even where I've gone quiet.

These small moments may feel ordinary—but they create the kind of soil where healing can finally take root.

A Prayer for Us

God,

Some parts of me have gone quiet. Others are sharp.

I want to stay soft—not just for myself, but for the people I love.

Gently till the places I've buried. Let Your mercy fall like rain.

Even when I don't feel it, help me believe You are still working the soil of my soul.

In Jesus' name, Amen.

A Prayer for the Weary

If this ache has lasted too long... this prayer is for you.

Heavenly Father,

For the ones who feel done—who haven't felt You in a long time—I ask for mercy. For the brittle places to soften.

For all who are weary and unsure how to move forward, till the soil of their hearts.

Not by force, but with kindness.

Let them feel again. Trust again.

Let them remember that You never left.

In Jesus' name, Amen.

What Happens When You Stay Soft

You begin to feel again. Not everything. Not all at once. But enough to notice the rain.

A woman once told me, "I started placing my hand over my heart each morning. I didn't know what I needed—but I knew I needed to stay open. Two months later, my daughter said, 'Mom, you're different.' That's when I knew—I was becoming soft again."

Even small shifts matter. Because when the heart stays soft, it becomes more than healed.

It becomes a place where others find safety too.

You don't have to force anything. Just begin again. One breath at a time. One layer at a time. And not just in you—but around you.

The silence becomes shelter. Your presence becomes peace. Your softness tells someone else they're safe to begin. Healing doesn't end with you—it begins to move through you.

Next, we'll explore what it means to become a safe place for others. Not by having answers—but by staying near. Because sometimes, the most healing thing we can offer is the sound of someone breathing beside us...and not leaving.

Chapter 18
Become a Safe Place

Rejoice with those who rejoice;
mourn with those who mourn.
—Romans 12:15—

Healing flows best where it isn't rushed.

There was a woman whose kitchen table became a sanctuary. She didn't quote many verses. She didn't rush to offer advice. She simply stayed.

People kept showing up. Not for answers, but for stillness. For presence. For a place where nothing had to be fixed to be holy.

She carried something rare: a quiet spirit that made others feel safe without feeling exposed.

Safe people offer space—not pressure.

Sometimes, the safest people are the ones who've done the deepest healing. They don't flinch at sorrow. They don't fill silence. They carry peace like a steady candle, offering warmth without burning too bright.

Who feels safe with you? What makes them feel that way?

The Quiet Power of Presence

Imagine sitting beside a quiet stream. No advice. No judgment. Just the sound of slow water, and the quiet shade of someone who isn't in a hurry.

Safe people are like that. Their presence doesn't perform. It surrounds.

Jesus was like that too. When Mary and Martha grieved, He didn't begin with a sermon. He didn't fix the pain. He felt it. He stayed. He wept.

Healing often begins in that kind of silence—the kind that reveres pain rather than solving it.

In many cultures, silence is sacred. A long pause can honor more than a thousand words. A slow nod. A still breath. A hand resting nearby. These are the liturgies of presence.

Healing isn't always something we say. Sometimes, it's something we hold. Sometimes, it's what we allow to remain unsaid.

Let that truth settle like water soaking into dry ground.

A Sacred Pause

You don't have to say the right thing.
You don't have to do the heavy lifting.

Being here—present, listening, gentle—is more powerful than you know.

So take a breath.

Let silence speak before you do.

Let love be felt before it's explained.

Jesus, slow my soul so I can simply stay.

When Helping Feels Heavy

Sometimes, after you listen to someone pour out their pain, you leave the conversation unsure. Did I help? Did I say too much? Too little?

You start replaying it all—the words, the pauses, the verses. It lingers heavy.

That doesn't mean you failed.

It might mean you carried more than you were meant to. It might mean you confused fixing with faithfulness.

Here are some signs you may be striving instead of staying:

- You speak too quickly, trying to ease discomfort
- You feel drained after conversations
- You wonder, "Did I say the right thing?"
- You replay the moment long after it ends

Instead of judging yourself, pause. Ask yourself gently:

- Do I feel emotionally safe with God right now?

- Am I creating room for silence in my own soul?
- Who do I trust to sit with me and not fix me?

Remember: we offer best what we've received first.
God's presence is always the beginning.

The Urge to Fix

It feels urgent to help, doesn't it?

To say the right verse. Offer the perfect prayer. Close the loop so the ache doesn't hang in the air too long.

But sometimes the most sacred gift is silence.

You're not doing nothing when you simply stay.
You're offering space for God to speak—for the ache to be seen.

Safe people don't rush pain.
They don't smother sorrow with solutions.
They make room for the ache to breathe.

They trust that presence, not pressure, is what heals.

A Spiritual Shift

Becoming a safe place isn't about mastering the perfect response.
It's about *slowing the soul.*

It's the courage to stay soft in a hard world.
It's choosing not to clean up someone else's sorrow.

It's letting the conversation stay tangled, the prayer stay unfinished, the tears stay messy.

It's giving grace the space to move before you do.

Jesus does this for you. Every day.

He stays through the panic. The numbness. The tangled, tear-soaked sentences that don't make sense.

He doesn't withdraw. He remains.

And now, because you've tasted that kind of mercy, you get to carry it. You become the calm corner in a chaotic room.

Not because you're strong.
But because you've been softened by grace.

Daily Rhythms of Sacred Stillness

You don't need a title to be a safe place.
You just need to slow down.

Try this today:

- *Pause before speaking.* Ask, "Jesus, how would You stay here?"
- *Listen for the ache beneath the words.*
- *Practice saying less.* Try, "That sounds really hard. I'm here."

It might feel small. But to someone whose world feels heavy, your presence becomes a warm chair pulled closer. A whisper of peace in a cold room.

You don't have to fix the moment.
You just have to stay with it.

Blessing Ritual

As someone shares this week, slow your spirit.
Don't rush to fill the air.
Just be.

And as you listen, pray quietly:
"You are safe here. God is near."

If welcomed, place a hand on their shoulder.
Not to guide. Not to fix. Just to remain.

Let your breath carry grace:
Inhale: *Jesus, You never rushed the hurting...*
Exhale: *...Teach me how to stay.*

This is holy presence:
Unhurried. Undistracted. Unshaken.

Sometimes, it's not what you say that makes a moment sacred.
It's how willing you are to remain.

A Prayer for Us

Lord,
I've rushed when I should have rested.
Spoken when I should have stayed still.
Slow me down.
Make my presence steady and kind.
Let me hold space the way You hold me—
with mercy, not fear.
Help me become a shelter for others,
just like You've been for me.
In Your name, Amen.

A Prayer for the One Who Wants to Stay

Jesus,

For every heart that longs to be a refuge—
but feels unsure or unworthy—I pray for grace.
For the ones who carry others but feel hollow inside,
let Your nearness refill what's run dry.

Let them know: just staying is enough.
Their silence can be sacred.
Their stillness can be healing.

And as they sit with sorrow that isn't theirs,
remind them that You sit beside them, too.

In Your name, Amen.

Becoming That Place

You don't need polished words to be a healing presence.

You just need to stay.

To breathe gently beside someone else's ache.

To carry peace instead of pressure.

To remain—when others rush away.

So pause.

Let that stillness settle in your soul.

Because the healing God started in you was never meant to stay hidden. It was meant to multiply.

In the warmth of a steady chair.

In the stillness between two breaths.

In a whispered prayer when words run out.

You are becoming a safe place.

Not by force.

But by presence.

And next, we'll look at how healing becomes legacy. Not because you were impressive. But because you stayed faithful.

Your presence tells a story. And someone near you is quietly hoping it might be true for them too.

.

Chapter 19
Pass It On

One generation will commend your works to another; they will tell of your mighty acts.

—Psalm 145:4—

You've faced the chains. You've walked the long road of healing. You've followed God through places you never thought you'd return from.

Now, your healing becomes a map someone else might follow.

A friend once whispered to me, "My grandfather never preached a sermon. But every time he prayed, I felt like heaven leaned in." She remembered how his presence steadied a room. His prayers were quiet, but they changed the atmosphere.

Years later, she finds herself whispering those same prayers over her own children. Not because he taught her. Because he lived it.

That's legacy.

It doesn't require a stage or a platform. It doesn't come after you're finished. It begins when you live whole in front of someone else—long enough for them to believe it's possible, too.

A Legacy That Grows Quietly

Legacy isn't what you leave behind—it's what quietly flows through you and beyond you.

Picture a river moving past your land. You can't see where it ends. It winds through forests and fields, nourishing places far beyond your reach.

That's what your story does when you surrender it to God. You may never know where it lands. But it flows. And it feeds.

There's a quiet lie many of us believe: *"My past disqualifies me from leaving anything good behind."*

Yet some of the deepest healing flows through the most broken places.

Healed people don't pass on perfection. They pass peace—and presence. And they point the way home.

What Legacy Looks Like

Legacy isn't always loud. Often, it whispers through daily acts of faithfulness:

- You stop hiding your limp.
- You speak from scars, not shame.
- You think more about those who come after you.

- You stop praying to impress. You start praying to be faithful.

Legacy isn't what you leave in writing. It's what you leave in someone's heart.

A woman who once struggled with self-doubt now mentors young girls, helping them recognize their worth.

A man who overcame addiction shares his story in prisons, offering hope and guidance to others still in bondage.

A couple who healed from infidelity now leads marriage workshops, equipping others to build resilient relationships.

Your wholeness has a ripple effect.

To own your healing doesn't mean to explain it. It means to hold it like a gift. No apologies. No editing. Just truth.

You're not just a survivor. You're a living seed—entrusted to bear fruit in others.

A Rhythm That Plants Seeds

Legacy is planted in ordinary soil. Try this rhythm this week:

- Each morning, ask: "Who might need what I've learned the hard way?"
- Bless one person with a note, a prayer, or a moment of presence.
- Begin the day with this breath prayer:

Inhale: God, plant something eternal in me...
Exhale: ...Let it grow through love.

And if your heart feels ready, write a letter.

Not a sermon. Just a note from your healing places—or even the ones still healing.

Write to your younger self—the version who needed a word, not a fix.

Or write to your children. To someone you haven't met yet.

What you write might become a lifeline. A root that grows underground until one day, it blooms where you least expect.

Ask yourself: What do I pray they carry forward?

Choose one word—*Gentle? Present? Honest? Brave? Safe? Whole?* Let that word shape how you live. And how you love.

A Quiet Inheritance

A missionary once told me, "My mother never told me how to be strong. I just watched her stay soft through the storms. That's why I believe in healing today. Because she didn't teach it—she lived it."

That's how legacy takes root.

Find a quiet place. Open your hands. Picture your story resting there—not fixed, not finished, just offered.

Say aloud: *"God, let my life be seed. Let it fall where You will."*

And let it go.

Tell someone: "I'm still becoming whole. But I want you to know what God is doing in me."

You're not passing on information. You're passing on hope.

Walking Home

This healing journey doesn't end here.

It continues—in every life you touch. In every prayer you leave behind. In every quiet act of presence that no one else may notice.

Healing multiplies when it's shared. It grows roots in conversations, in gentle encouragement, in the space you create just by showing up.

Wholeness becomes legacy when it walks beside someone else. When your story becomes a bridge, and your scars become a light.

The seed you plant today may become the shade someone else rests under tomorrow.

And maybe they'll never know it was you—but heaven will.

A Prayer for the One Who Wants to Leave a Legacy

Almighty God,

I don't feel impressive. I don't feel finished.

But I want to live in a way that helps someone else breathe easier.

Use what You've healed in me—and what You're still healing—to open doors for others.

Let my scars tell the story of Your mercy. Let my presence carry peace.

Let my story point to You.

And for those coming behind me—those like [insert name]—may they find healing in our stories, witness lives transformed by grace, and walk paths of wholeness we've begun to clear.

Let my life be seed—quiet, steady, and real.

In Jesus' name, Amen

Epilogue
The Journey That Doesn't End

You've come far. You've named what bound you. You've walked into rooms where the air once trembled with fear—places your soul never thought it would return to. You didn't rush. You surrendered, one slow step at a time.

You found the key. You turned the handle. You opened the door.

And now—healing is no longer a single event. It's a rhythm. A way of walking with God through every season, shadow, and silence.

The weight will still return some days—grief, memory, or an ache with no name. There may still be moments when pain whispers, *"You're not really free."*

But now you know better.

You know the Gardener returns again and again. You've seen how silence can hold the holy. You've felt Jesus stay—even when others left. Even when you didn't have words. Even when all you could do was breathe.

Healing is no longer only for you—it's becoming what God does through you. Every day you choose presence over pressure.

Every time you stay open instead of shutting down. Every moment you become a safe place for someone else.

This journey doesn't end with your story.

Think of one person—someone still standing outside a locked door. Still unsure if healing could be for them. Still wondering if freedom has a name.

Let your story become a key. Let your presence be a warm light in their hallway. Walk with them—not as their guide, but as a quiet echo of the grace that carried you.

If these words have held you, pass them on. Not as a solution—but as a signpost. A whispered reminder: *"There's a way through."*

You don't need to be perfect. You don't need a platform. You just need to be willing.

You're ready—even if you don't feel ready.

Walk beside someone the way Jesus has walked with you.

And watch healing begin again—in them, in you, in the space between.

A Final Blessing

Before you go, receive this blessing.
Not a finish line—
but a quiet planting.
The beginning of something holy beneath the surface.
A sign that you are no longer just surviving,
but growing.

A reminder of who you're becoming—
and of the healing you now carry like a lantern into dark places.
You're not just leaving this book—you're walking forward with grace at your side.

May you breathe deeply of God's kindness—
not once, but often.
Let it be slow. Steady. Enough for this moment.

May the soil of your soul stay soft—especially on the days that feel dry,
especially when silence stretches longer than you wanted.

May you open the doors of your heart—
even the rooms where the air still feels heavy—
and welcome Jesus into every corner,
without rushing Him to tidy anything.

You are not too broken.

You are becoming whole.

And this healing?

It will not end with you.

If your heart feels ready, whisper this:
"Lord, I'm still healing—but I'm also ready to help someone else home."

Write down one word—
the one you pray your legacy will whisper.
Let it be your stone of remembrance.
A quiet altar.
A marker of where healing deepened and hope took root.

And as you take that next step,
carry this promise with you:

You will be called Repairer of Broken Walls,
Restorer of Streets with Dwellings.
—Isaiah 58:12

You've never walked alone.
And you don't have to be finished to be faithful.

Just keep the soil soft—
and the door open.

And when someone else is ready…
take their hand…
and help them walk home, too.

Thank You

If you've made it to this page, I want to pause and say—thank you. Not just for reading, but for walking this road with me. You didn't just flip pages. You opened doors. You stepped into rooms of memory, ache, and possibility. You chose to stay soft when it would've been easier to shut down.

That matters. It means more than you know. This book wasn't written from a mountaintop. It came from the valleys—mine and many others. So if it brought light to one of your dark corners, I give God the thanks. And if it nudged you closer to healing, to Jesus, to peace—then I rejoice with you.

If these words helped you breathe easier, would you share that with someone else?

Your voice could be the very thing that helps someone else find the courage to begin. Sometimes all it takes is a whisper from someone who's been there.

Thank you again, friend.
Let's keep walking—healed, whole, and unbroken. Together.

About the Author

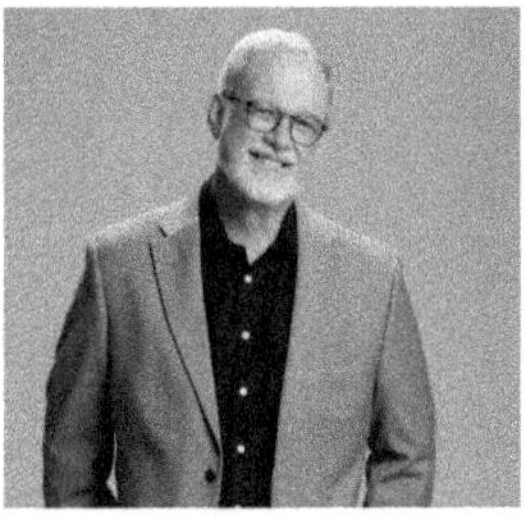

Dr. Daniel B. Lancaster doesn't come with all the answers—just a heart that's been learning to listen.

For years, he has served in ministry, trained leaders, and quietly battled the same soul loops this book now names. He knows what it's like to love Jesus deeply but still wrestle with anxiety, shame, fear, and exhaustion. This book isn't written from a mountaintop. It's written from the valley—where grace shows up most faithfully.

He believes healing begins with honesty, that surrender is stronger than striving, and that the gospel isn't a ladder to climb but a place to rest.

Today, Dr. Dan helps others step out of their silent spirals and into the kind of freedom that doesn't require performance—just presence. His greatest joy isn't in being impressive. It's in being real.

He's most at home when he's listening—whether to the Holy Spirit, a hurting friend, or the kind of silence where God speaks softest.

He wrote this book for anyone who feels stuck but still believes in grace. Because he's one of them.

www.ingramcontent.com/pod-product-compliance
Lightning Source LLC
LaVergne TN
LVHW051402080426
835508LV00022B/2934